Negotiat   7

SELF-DEVELOPMENT FOR MANAGERS

A major series of workbooks for managers edited by Jane Cranwell-Ward.

This series presents a selection of books in workbook format, on a range of key management issues and skills. The books are designed to provide practising managers with the basis for self-development across a wide range of industries and occupations.

Each book relates to other books in the series to provide a coherent new approach to self-development for managers. Closely based on the latest management training initiatives, the books are designed to complement management development programmes, in-house company training, and the management qualification programmes such as CMS, DMS, MBA and professional qualification programmes.

Other books in the series:

Thriving on Stress
Jane Cranwell-Ward

Accounting for Managers
Roger Oldcorn

Managing Change
Colin Carnall

Developing Assertiveness
Anni Townend

Effective Problem Solving
Dave Francis

The Self-reliant Manager
Chris Bones

Step-by-step Competitive Strategy
Dave Francis

Effective Marketing
Geoffrey Randall

Improving Environmental Performance
Suzanne Pollack

Developing the Manager as a Helper
John Hayes

The New Flexi-manager
David Birchall

Making Sense of the Economy
Roger Martin-Fagg

Managing International Business
Neil Coade

Jane Cranwell-Ward is at Henley Management College. She is the author of *Managing Stress* (Pan, 1986).

Negotiating the Better Deal

Peter Fleming

Managing Partner,
Peter Fleming Associates,
Oxfordshire.

INTERNATIONAL THOMSON BUSINESS PRESS
I ⓣ P An International Thomson Publishing Company

London • Bonn • Boston • Johannesburg • Madrid • Melbourne • Mexico City • New York • Paris
Singapore • Tokyo • Toronto • Albany, NY • Belmont, CA • Cincinnati, OH • Detroit, MI

Negotiating the Better Deal

Copyright © 1997 Peter Fleming

First published by International Thomson Business Press

I(T)P A division of International Thomson Publishing Inc.
The ITP logo is a trademark under licence

British Library Cataloguing-in-Publication Data
A catalogue record for this book is available from the British Library

---

First edition 1997

Typeset by Photoprint, Torquay, Devon
Printed in the UK by Clays Ltd, St Ives plc, Suffolk

ISBN 0–41512–567–7

International Thomson Business Press
Berkshire House
168–173 High Holborn
London WC1V 7AA
UK

International Thomson Business Press
20 Park Plaza
13th Floor
Boston MA 02116
USA

http://www.itbp.com

— *Contents*

— *Series editor's preface*

The last decade has been a time of tremendous change, impacting on organizations and their employees. Managers have seen organizations become leaner and less bureaucratic, to enable them to cope with a more turbulent environment and increased competition. Organizations have delayered and the tight functional boundaries have disappeared. Managers are often required to participate in a range of different teams and need work done by people who are not their direct reports.

As a result of these changes, managers need to adopt different approaches and styles and build up a new set of skills to be able to meet the challenges which face them. Negotiating is one of these skills. Ten years ago, only managers at a very senior level, or those in a sales or procurement role would have been trained to negotiate. Today, most managers recognize the importance of being able to negotiate effectively either from a contractual or from a relationship perspective as part of fulfilling a mangerial role. The skill also has importance outside work.

Negotiating the Better Deal has been written for those who have already acquired the basic skills of negotiating and need to enhance these skills to perform more effectively. Once readers have tested their assumptions of the nature of negotiating they will be able to assess their current skill level and identify ways of enhancing performance. The book then offers a systematic approach to be followed in order to become a successful negotiator. The book also offers advice on team negotiations.

Completion of practical assignments are an essential component of the book. Without applying the ideas and lessons learnt there is little chance of improving performance. 'Experience should be lived, not dreamed about.' Managers are also encouraged to seek feedback from others as part of the learning process, and to see learning as continuous with regular reviews for improvement.

Peter Fleming, the author of *Negotiating the Better Deal*, has over twenty years of experience training managers to develop their negotiating skills. I have known Peter throughout that time and thought that his approach would be ideal for the Self Development Series. Peter has his own consultancy and negotiation skills training is a core part of his business.

The Self Development Series has been written to enable managers to face the future with greater confidence. It aims to address personal skills such as stress, assertiveness and time management, and business capability including finance and marketing. It also helps managers contribute more strategically by developing an understanding of the economic environment, international business and competitor analysis.

Jane Cranwell-Ward
Series Editor

— *Introduction*

Negotiation has been described variously as *frustrating, fascinating, fun, frivolous* or *fumbling*, but rarely **boring**! I hope that my underlying fascination, with the ways in which people work together whilst constructing their deals, shines through the text of this book; sharing this with you, the reader, was one of my main motivations in writing it.

I would like to record here my gratitude to the thousands of executives and managers I have met on our public workshops and training seminars. Whilst helping them to develop their skills, they have contributed to my understanding of the key issues in various marketplaces – and some valuable experiences and case studies. I hope that those illustrations we have been able to include help the reader to understand the principles involved in achieving 'better deals'. My thanks are also due to Jane Cranwell-Ward for her continuing encouragement for me to complete the project and to Terry and our family for their forbearance while I did it!

The self-development element of this book will help the 'learner' to apply the text. However, practice makes perfect and a practical workshop (preferably including video-coaching techniques) will help cement the skills elements. Perhaps we will meet on a workshop in the future. (More details of this service are available from us on 01235 534124).

Finally, may I wish you good fortune with all your endeavours.

Peter Fleming
PFA, Oxfordshire
1997

1 *What you will be able to achieve from this book*

INTRODUCTION

This book is deliberately written for the negotiator who has already explored the subject – maybe read a 'primer' on the subject – or has been coached on-the-job by a more capable colleague. It has been prepared to answer the questions of achievers – those who *know* that there are better ways to obtain an edge in deals – but somehow find that the necessary skills elude them.

Having attended some previous formal negotiation training session will help the reader grasp the issues – but, even more important, is having the drive to put this text to work after reading it. Two factors will help with this:

- **the assignments** – which are designed to help readers apply the thinking to their own worlds;
- **attending a structured learning workshop** – which includes some video coaching.

Negotiation has become a topical issue. Referred to by Prime Ministers and Presidents, blamed when things go wrong, and used as a diplomatic tactic by nations when trying to bring local wars to an end, most industrialists have identified negotiation skills as a major contributor to the 'bottom line' and objectives of an enterprise. Throughout difficult periods of recession, senior managers, key account executives and purchasing managers have been trained and briefed to achieve much 'sharper' deals as overheads have had to be trimmed, service levels enhanced and profit margins protected.

How has this situation arisen?

Negotiation has traditionally been seen as a skill – based on special qualities, or power, which was frequently practised between senior executives, diplomats etc. (or 'consenting adults') in privacy! We might suspect that this was deliberate – so that lesser mortals never witnessed the methods in use and how the 'mystique' attached to the label 'top negotiator' was maintained.

Today, charismatic leaders – jetting from capital to capital – carry the hopes and fears of whole continents with them as they seek to find compromises in tariff-free trade, East/West disarmament, and lasting peace in situations of conflict.

Undoubtedly, the famous quotation (by Sir Winston Churchill, during the 'Cold War'), 'To jaw-jaw is better than to war-war', offers much to the diplomat and emissary – but does it have anything to offer business executives?

There *is* usually a time when the talking has to stop and must be superseded by action! The world of business is generally driven by a need to achieve results – production, sales, reports, services and – most important of all – profits! Negotiation skills are just one more important element in managers' toolboxes to help them achieve these results.

So what of the future?

Negotiation is one of the last skills *not* to be outmoded by high technology. The world has appeared to become a smaller place – international travel has speeded up and some of it has even been made unnecessary as information can be transmitted around the world through such devices as the Internet – and teleconferencing has even made 'electronic negotiating' possible.

So, what is so special about the negotiation meeting?
Why are 'summit meetings' still held?

It would be easy to forget that influencing someone else is always easier face to face than it might be over the telephone (or fax). Regardless of how poorly we 'read' the body language of others, mostly we feel that we are better able to build up an understanding with suppliers, clients, advisers and even adversaries, when we meet them face to face.

The pace of modern-day life can make speculative meetings appear to be something of a luxury and yet it is clear that 'pressing the flesh' has always been effective, *and probably always will be.*

So, negotiation is here to stay and most of us *have* to become better at it if we are to obtain every ounce of effectiveness out of what we do!

Does this mean more pressure, stress or personality changes are likely to result? Decidedly no!

As this book will show, a structured approach to negotiation will bring a rapid improvement in results for most people – and some may go on to become 'masters' at it.

A MODEL FOR LEARNING

Everybody has their own individual style of learning – and this explains why some people find it easier to learn from formal workshops or through self-development methods such as open learning and studying texts such as this one. These concepts arise from the work of Kolb, who identified the following learning sequence:

- **Conceptualizing**: grasping theories and concepts which, if applied, should assist the learner in the job.
- **Experimenting**: trying out ideas in practice – almost by trial and error.
- **Experiencing**: building up a body of experience which contributes to our understanding of what works in practice.
- **Evaluating**: learning by observing and analysing the activities of others (or perhaps oneself via video recordings etc.).

So, what this indicates is that some of us gain more from practical experimentation, or observation, than, say, direct lectures. In fact, most negotiation skills workshops aim to produce a blend of learning methods – ensuring that all participants gain from the event.

Clearly, negotiation skills are essentially practical in nature, and are unlikely to be successfully developed without an element of practical development; this underlines the importance of the assignments in this text which are deliberately provided to help the reader apply the concepts involved. The learner will also benefit from access to other 'negotiators' – perhaps a colleague or boss who should be able to endorse or counsel on the assignments carried out.

LEVELS OF EXPERIENCE AND DEVELOPMENT

Negotiating is a skill which most of us learned by trying to obtain extensions to the bedtime 'deadline' from our parents, more sweets from grandparents or inclusion in the sports team at school; some of us were better at it than others – and so it is in adult life.

However, capability does *not* necessarily depend on seniority or even levels of exposure. Very senior executives have been known to make *very* expensive mistakes – just like their more junior colleagues; sometimes the rush to close a deal can bring disaster in company takeovers – just as in buying the 'wrong' secondhand car. We all make mistakes from time to time and this applies to negotiation, as in many other fields. However, it is essential that we learn from our mistakes *and avoid repeating them.*

A SYSTEMATIC APPROACH TO NEGOTIATION SKILLS DEVELOPMENT

This book assumes that the reader is able to identify his or her own strengths and weaknesses in negotiating. Some people find this harder than others – and those who find it hardest may find it useful to consult with trusted 'advisers' at work (or at home). Seeing ourselves as others do is not always as easy as it sounds – nor always very pleasant. Several of the assignments in the text will benefit from this kind of comparison and feedback – and many valuable insights should be gained from the process.

Aiming at a systematic approach to developing the skills described in the book assumes that the following process has been undertaken – or can be completed as part of the implementation process.

THE SYSTEMATIC DEVELOPMENT PROCESS

❏ Performance standards have been set (both by individuals and their organizations).

❏ Assessment has been made against these standards (through a formal appraisal process or by informal performance counselling.

❏ Specific improvement areas are identified.

❏ Coaching or training is provided to fill the gap.

❏ Further evaluations or appraisals are made to check on progress and ensure that performance has not slipped back to the 'old ways'.

There are two challenges in this process.

(a) **Negotiation skills impact directly on results** achieved inside the organization; this can lead to corners being cut or even unethical methods being adopted – at either company or individual levels. The most professionally run organizations are those which have adopted a culture which has established 'ways of doing things'. Cutting corners in such organizations – once discovered – will definitely be frowned upon, and may even earn disciplinary action. So, the moulding of attitudes – from the corporate viewpoint – is especially important for negotiators; failure to do this risks a patchwork quilt of individual styles and methods which have been embroidered from past experiences and achievements.

(b) **In increasingly tough economic climates**, pressure builds up for negotiators to achieve even better results. This pressure can lead to individuals paying less regard for longer-term effects of deals because of the need to achieve short-term results. The natural consequence of this can be the complete abandonment of integrity or even a win/win philosophy. Several sectors of industry have experienced these challenges and are still trying to find a way out of the win/lose culture.

An alternative argument advanced by believers of a totally free market maintains that high achiever negotiators are still relatively 'rare animals' and ought to be employable for the results they can achieve – regardless of the methods or styles they might adopt. Some readers of this book might feel themselves to be in this category. However, the world changes – and old methods may not necessarily fit us for the future market conditions. Hence the various references to 'lifelong learning'; we all need to make a conscious effort to keep the learning process going – long after we have reached the performance standards which seem to enable us to achieve the 'better win/win deals' which this book seeks to encourage.

LOOKING AHEAD

The following chapters offer a sequenced approach to the topic and the case for improving skills is repeated in each chapter – in various ways. We move through the following sequence:

Chapter	Theme/Skill
2	Testing our perceptions of Negotiation
3	The skills audit – identifying development needs
4	The structured approach – introducing PROD-ProSC
5	Preparation and Research – setting out the standards
6	Opening and orchestrating the discussion – how to use and resist persuasion skills used at the start of the meeting
7	Proposals and persuasion skills – how to move the meeting forward
8	Team negotiation – how to avoid the common pitfalls
9	Conflict – how it arises and how to prepare for handling it
10	Closing skills – how to bring the meeting to a close

Chapter 2 encourages the reader to test perceptions of what negotiation is really about – the results of this may be surprising – and the time investment involved may alarm some readers!

Chapter 3 provides not one, but two skills audits – the first for those readers who have not explored the subject in much depth until reading this book. The second is intended for those who already have considerable negotiating experience and are looking for ways of bringing their skills up to an 'advanced' level.

Chapter 4 sets out a systematic approach to negotiation meetings using a mnemonic – PROD-ProSC – and explains why skilled negotiators may move away from structured meetings. The review assignment encourages the reader to put the framework into practice with a real-life task.

Chapters 5 to 7 and 10 are designed to help readers apply the individual components of the framework in a more systematic way – giving due concern to some of the pitfalls which they may already have experienced. In each case, emphasis is placed upon phraseology, tactics and how to use persuasive skills (as well as highlighting the behaviours rejected by skilled negotiators).

Chapter 8 provides some useful tips and advice on team negotiation – often used by experienced negotiators but rarely covered in training materials or workshops. Emphasis is given to the preparation and practice dimension.

Chapter 9 includes an innovative exploration of conflict issues – how they arise and how to prepare for handling them.

Chapter 11 provides some reminders about the most important facet of negotiation – the implementation phase – which is what the whole process is all about (!) and the last chapter sets out to tempt the reader to embrace those concepts of lifelong learning about negotiation which we mentioned above.

All-in-all the reader should find the modular approach presented by the text will enable the concepts and techniques to be tried on a sequential basis, spread over a reasonable time period.

TOWARDS A 'BETTER DEAL' – DREAM OR REALITY?

Have you ever found yourself reviewing 'deals' which may have been applied in your domestic life?

The kind of statement made may have been, 'Do you know, that was the best decision we ever took – buying that particular washing machine/dishwasher/car' etc.

With all the consumer advice, surveys and protection schemes, it often seems that some domestic purchases can be a lottery, so it is hardly surprising that the same kind of feeling can sometimes be left after a particularly difficult negotiating decision has been taken – and, in retrospect, we can apply the same criteria; would I do that again? If not, there was clearly some influence at work which I did not recognize at the time or perhaps, if it proved to be a really good decision, I failed to exploit it as much as I should have done.

So, we *can* identify the 'better deals'. The question is: can we work harder towards achieving them *more of the time* and, if so, can we build a really impressive track record of success so that we can achieve better results and a really good reputation for our organization and ourselves?

Clearly, this is both possible and desirable – many people have applied it *and* made it work. Only the reader will be able to put this objective at the top of the daily 'to do' checklist and endeavour to achieve such a result. If this book enables more people to do this, then it will have achieved its purpose. Good luck with your endeavours!

2 Negotiation – what does it really mean?

INTRODUCTION

This chapter is intended to test the reader's perception of what negotiation is really about. From a 'textbook definition' we identify different cultures in which negotiation takes place, consider when it may become necessary, and advise on some of the options available. Since the practice of negotiation is interactive it is essential for us to start out with a clear understanding of what *we mean* by the words – because it may be that our 'partners' turn out to have a rather different understanding of the processes and desired outcomes.

The *Oxford English Dictionary* shows the following definition: 'Negotiate – To confer with another with an intention to compromise or reach agreement.' We are immediately challenged with experiences of meetings which demonstrated few (if any) of these characteristics. To be precise:

Confer

■ **Have you ever attended a meeting in which the other party clearly had the intention to 'tell' you what to do – or what they wanted?** What opportunity was there for genuine conferring? And how did you feel about it? True negotiation will only really take place when both parties feel that they have an adequate opportunity to discuss or debate the issues.

Another

■ **How often do you negotiate with more than one party at a time?** The idea of two persons attending the meeting from your opponent's side can be somewhat intimidating (and does give some advantages and disadvantages – as we will see) but these reactions can be controlled. What should be avoided is the unwitting negotiating with *several interested parties* – all together in the same room; a kind of United Nations meeting in which set speeches may be made and everyone is learning tactics from witnessing the behaviour of all your 'opponents' and *your* reactions. Most skilled negotiators avoid this scenario if at all possible.

Intention

■ **Have you ever been called to a meeting, only to discover that the client or supplier subsequently lost interest in closing a deal?** Most of us have had this happen to us at some time or another and may have spent some hours wondering, after the event, just what we did wrong that the other party had become reluctant to close the deal.

Apart from the possibilities that the client or supplier did not value our offers (and related benefits) after all – and perhaps did not warm to ourselves, either – the fact is that the other party's **intention** to reach agreement was missing. This raises the possibility that they were really only 'window shopping' and that the timing of the meeting was not right. We are all active participants in window shopping in our domestic lives; we gaze through shop windows and make plans, we may even visit shops and test out the product knowledge of salespeople – but still walk out without buying anything. The sales staff have to recognize such visitors as **potential** customers who often put off a buying decision with some such statement as 'I'll think about it'.

It could be said that the salesperson failed to create sufficient **buyer motivation** to encourage the customer but we just know that we often use shopping as a leisure activity ('one of these days we'll buy one of those', we might say). It can be the same in a negotiation and either party may need to test out their opponent's strength of desire to reach an agreement today.

Compromise

So, compromise is the final element in the definition:

■ **When you attend negotiating meetings, do you have the feeling that you are the only person who seems interested in reaching a compromise? Or perhaps you shut out all thoughts of 'second best' and go for achieving all your objectives with little hint of**

any flexibility? Generally, the process of negotiation demands some flexibility from either party – it is unlikely that both parties will achieve 100 per cent of their objectives without the other party incurring some 'loss' of some kind. Would *you* not feel some nervousness about an opponent who agreed to make all the concessions with little in return; perhaps they might be desperate for a deal (?); and why could that be (?); maybe their service/product/ members are not as good as they claim!

The great 'British compromise' may not be a good advertisement for negotiation. One famous prime minister made public her scorn for the 'fudge' factor, and the British do have a strong regard for 'fair play', 'sticking to the rules', and the idea of 'cricket'. Whilst this is not actually wrong – it might blind us to identifying correct objectives to try to achieve in a negotiation meeting – and, more importantly, the strength of argument to be advanced in support of each separate objective. When examined from this perspective, concessions should only be seen to be 'fair' when they are earned and defended with some objective reasoning (for example their comparative value to either of the parties involved). We will return to this issue in chapter 7.

INFLUENCE IN NEGOTIATION

Influencing someone else in a negotiation meeting is often dependent upon two factors:

- **benefits** and
- **trust**.

There is little point in setting up a meeting unless either (or preferably both) of the parties recognize that there are benefits to be gained from it. However, these perceived benefits need to be appreciated by the other party or they are worthless and, what is more, the meeting will only be effective if a condition of trust exists between the two parties. So, trust and integrity affect results; and so, too, do some other much more subjective issues.

However hard we try to pretend to be totally objective, the average human being is really quite subjective – especially in our likes and dislikes. Try this short exercise.

ASSIGNMENT 1: LIKES AND DISLIKES

Looking back at your recent negotiation experiences try to bring to mind two contrasting 'opponents'. The first was someone who, no matter how hard you tried, you just seemed unable to 'warm to'. You really would not care if you never saw that person again – ever!

The other person you took to almost immediately – he or she made the meeting enjoyable and you would be very happy to do business with them again! Now try to complete the table below using ticks (where you feel you would be supportive) and crosses (where you might be tempted to be negative).

Your reactions to . . . ?	'Warm' feelings in meeting	'Cold' feelings in meeting
Your determination to achieve your own objectives		
Your interest in the other party's objectives		
Your determination to gain concessions		
Your preparedness to make concessions		
Your preparedness to build up trust of you by your opponent		
Your trust of the other party		

Your willingness to attend a further meeting		

You may have found from this simple exercise that we really are not quite as objective as we would like to pretend and you can be pretty sure that, if your reactions to others affect the ultimate deal you achieve, the same is probably true of how others see *you*.

If you would like to achieve **better deals** – as the book title suggests – then the best starting-point lies with you. This chapter is a deliberate attempt to test our perceptions of *what negotiation is* – and what it definitely *is not*!

PERCEPTIONS OF NEGOTIATION

So, from a simple definition, we find that our perceptions of negotiation shift depending upon the quality or value of the deals we are achieving. If *you* are constantly 'winning' you might have bought this book with the intention of finding out how to stay ahead. The question is, how might your current 'opponents' feel about that? If your 'wins' are *too great*, you might find them seeking alternative clients, suppliers or employers with whom they might prefer to do business.

If, on the other hand, you are dissatisfied with the agreements you are achieving – or are fairly certain you could do better – then you might need to consider the level of trading you might need to do in order to achieve a '**better deal**'. We will review the methods you should consider in chapter 7.

Negotiation holds a certain fascination because it crosses the boundaries of culture and business. Most people in Europe have an implicit sense that business deals should achieve a win/win result; that business really needs longer-term relationships growing from collaborative partnerships since these build goodwill and grow the mutual businesses of those organizations involved. There are, in fact, three cultures of negotiation which may reflect the world zones of the players – but more frequently describe the business culture of each organization.

Competitive

Competitive business cultures are very noticeably American in origin. Success is all (usually measured in financial terms) and, at its most extreme, is uncaring of whether the opponent achieves success or not. This is rarely as unpleasant as a determination to win *at the expense of the other player* but often is associated with the notion that it is the other party's responsibility to look after their own needs – and not your task. This form of bargaining is common in American business – but can also be identified all over the world. A sales negotiator in Neasden may prove to be just as competitive as a key account executive in Nebraska. Is this wrong?

The answer lies in the *quality of the deals which have been transacted.* If either party becomes dissatisfied with the results of the negotiations – aware perhaps that they have been 'stitched up' in some way – then the *implementation* of the arrangements may prove less than satisfactory. One-off deals with competitive negotiators can carry quite a lot of risk – because of the lack of any controlling influences on the outcome and subsequent implementation.

CASE HISTORY

A UK public company wished to sell its training centre – a listed building in the leafy shires. Prospective purchasers were invited to make sealed bids following their visits to the property. One tenderer was particularly taken by the unique collection of pictures which were exhibited in the main house – and also the opportunities presented by the house, and other buildings close by, for conversion into a hotel. They achieved a great success with their bid which was accepted quickly but, unfortunately, they failed to take adequate advice. The price paid (substantially higher than the nearest bids) had not included the picture collection – a fact they only realized when they took possession. Furthermore, their hotel plans were thwarted by the very stringent planning rules applied by the local planning authorities. There was no hint of any malpractice – simply a win/lose deal. The client had made some wrong assumptions.

Better deals are made by negotiators who scrutinise *all* the small print!

Consensus

The Far East is known for a consensus business culture and Japanese businesses, in particular, are known for their strong desire to understand the motives and business cultures of suppliers, main clients and 'partners'. Many a sales executive has experienced the painful business (to them) of having to pass over numbers of 'hurdles' or 'beauty shows' which are erected by Japanese executives who are simply trying to get to know all the ins and outs of their partners. This process can take a substantial number of meetings, and those seeking success in Japan must be prepared to invest much time (and money) in creating positive relationships – before contracts are drafted and exchanged. The problem with this style of business (from the European perspective) is that it can be exceptionally slow. The British have become accustomed to one or two meetings resulting in a contract – the longer-term relationships between the parties may not have been considered carefully but then 'the contract can always be cancelled, can't it?' So, a distinct difference of culture can result here and, whilst consensus negotiation should achieve win/win in the long run, it can also result in a lose/lose outcome if it is insufficiently responsive to immediate events and opportunities.

CASE HISTORY

A leading British plc wished to sell its automotive subsidiary and raise some much needed cash. This was not a secret and it was courting potential purchasers leading, eventually, to an attractive bid from a top European manufacturer. At short notice, the plc consulted their Japanese partners to see if they wished to make a counter-bid. The Japanese company was not pleased with the pressure to piece together their bid in such a short time and, when it was made, it included only part of the total business which was for sale. The sale was made to the European business – to the somewhat undiplomatic glee of some elements of the British media who interpreted the deal as a 'put-down' for Japanese business. Time will tell who made the best deal.

The best deals stand the ultimate test of time!

Collaborative

As has already been discussed, the search for win/win deals with both parties seeking to build a supportive relationship – or partnership – assumes a strong desire to achieve a lasting kinship which will survive the natural difficulties which may arise from time to time. Many words have been used to describe this 'desirable' condition but, in practice, the real test of a truly collaborative relationship occurs over the issue of information. The healthiest family relationships occur when secrets are not kept from family members – and strong feelings of trust and openness pervade the atmosphere.

Clearly, these conditions are built up and emphasized over a period of time and can be jeopardized by short-term gains by either side – or perhaps the replacement of a collaborative negotiator by a competitive one. Ultimately, trust built up over years can be destroyed in hours by just one deal motivated by greed or short-termism.

CASE HISTORY

A British food retailer – known for the strongly competitive behaviour of its buying team – endeavoured to change its image through a series of negotiation skills training workshops. Delegates were well briefed and exposed this ambition to their fellow course members at the start of the programmes. They sat attentively through the explanation of collaborative behaviour and showed great interest in the ways of achieving win/win deals. When it came to role-play exercises, however, each delegate showed strong leanings towards win/lose, competitive behaviour (strongly endorsed by their opponents who felt they had been 'stitched-up'). Two morals arise from this example:

Changing from competitive behaviour to collaborative behaviour in negotiation requires more than a simple statement of intent!

Old habits die hard – especially when the negotiator senses an open goal or an element of weakness in the opponent's arguments!

It should be said that being collaborative in a negotiation does not imply any sense of being 'nice', 'weak' or 'compliant'. Collaborative negotiators stick up for their positions just as any other negotiator might. The principal difference is that they look for opportunities to trade-off their objectives and concessions '*quid pro quo*' or 'something for something'.

WHEN IS NEGOTIATION NECESSARY

Experienced negotiators quickly recount lists of situations in which they are able to use their skills. On public workshops, delegates categorize the amount of time they spend on negotiation from a low category (0–20 per cent) to a high category (80–100 per cent). Those who fall into the lowest category usually occupy quiet, undemanding roles with infrequent contact with clients or suppliers (possibly working on their own with little or no staff responsibility) and in markets with little change or affectation from economic pressures. Those who operate at the highest levels are regularly trying to influence the direction of their organizations and those of their partners outside – and probably enjoy the high level of exposure. In fact, high-profile negotiators often recount how greater practice of the skills encourages them to be using the skills in **increasing** situations – both at work and in their domestic lives. They become **instinctive negotiators** – they enjoy it and, of course, become better at it. We could divide negotiation opportunities into three groups:

■ Fiscal opportunities
■ Occupational opportunities
■ Instinctive opportunities

Fiscal opportunities

As the name implies, these are regular opportunities driven by the need to respond to a systemized way of running the business. For example:

– the negotiation round involved in drawing up, and having approved, operating budgets;
– the annual round of pay bargaining;
– the annual review of price lists or contract terms.

These opportunities are usually accompanied by much serious preparation and planning – budgeting – and briefing, before the actual negotiation meetings take place. This might even include the rehearsal of the case in a role-playing environment.

Most participants in this form of negotiation are only given the authority to negotiate at this level after some time spent working alongside a senior executive – and learning by observation and example. (This is not to replace formal learning but it does ensure that all the key players are working to similar 'rules', parameters and styles.)

Occupational opportunities

These are represented by the direct responsibilities contained in the occupations of buying, selling and staff relations. Bargaining at this level will usually become 'honed' by normal practice in the particular market in which we operate. For example, in the fast-moving consumer goods markets, pressures on margins, space and time can be quite intense – leading to quite a lot of competitive behaviour. By contrast, negotiating in the arts can be quite relaxed and dependent more on personal relationships than direct and short-term results.

Instinctive opportunities

These are the opportunities which occur almost by accident – the negotiation of free refreshments when a train or plane is delayed, the seeking of a better seat when there has been some confusion over reservations in the theatre. Once again, the style of bargaining will vary in different situations. For example, the angry customer may provide an impressive 'lever' in the foyer of a restaurant where any number of expectant diners are present but a real row may cause the customer's partner to lose his or her appetite and enjoyment for the evening.

ASSIGNMENT 2: SKILLS AND OUTCOMES AUDIT

The following table will help you define some of your goals for improving your negotiation skills.

When you have completed the table, you might seek confirmation of the evidence from someone who knows you well – at home or at work. Try to identify specific cases in support of your ratings.

Type of negotiation	Approximate time spent (%)	Satisfied with current outcomes	Some improvement of outcomes is possible	Major improvement of outcomes is possible
Fiscal				
Occupational				
Instinctive				

THE FASCINATION OF NEGOTIATION

So what is so fascinating about negotiation? The fact is that results from a negotiation may be quite difficult to predict. How can it be that two different teams of negotiatiors working on identical facts, can arrive at sometimes quite different outcomes. The fact is that we are describing an activity which is dependent on interpretation of data and, ultimately, the varying ability of one person to persuade another of the strength of his or her case. These are skills which employers and clients are prepared to pay for quite handsomely; and it is easy to see why.

Just supposing you were arrested in the street with considerable circumstantial evidence which linked you to an appalling crime – perhaps a particularly gruesome murder. Denied bail, because of the seriousness of the case and the apparent weight of the evidence against you, you would wish to have a QC present the case of your innocence in the most persuasive way possible. In fact you would probably spare no expense to employ the very best advocate possible. A case like this really concentrates the mind. How do *your* skills of persuasion square up to the sense of mission you would expect from the advocate in this hypothetical case?

Scientists and statisticians sometimes find the imprecision of the skills and qualities we are describing here as rather irritating. After all, $2 + 2 = 4$ and there is little point in trying to debate the fact. However, we can all think of situations in which, for very good reason, we might wish to present a case in which the facts can be turned to our advantage – in business or at home.

CASE HISTORY

The owner of a cottage sited alongside a busy main road was rather pessimistic about the prospects of selling it because of the noise of the traffic outside. Expecting to have to make a concession on the selling price, he was somewhat amazed to be offered the asking price by a blind man and his wife. In casual conversation – after the offer had been accepted – the client revealed that he had only recently lost his sight and welcomed the external noise because, as he said, 'It reminds me that there is a real world, with real activity outside.'

One person's needs may reveal another person's opportunities.

TO NEGOTIATE OR NOT TO NEGOTIATE?

Negotiation is often associated with considerations of power. Power of one person or organization over another may be misused and cause a win/lose outcome – and there are plenty of examples in history of this. (For example, the Allies imposition of punitive damages on Germany after World War I which was felt by some to have contributed towards the causes of World War II.)

The advantage of establishing a 'custom and practice' way of handling changing circumstances between the players is that bad surprises can be avoided. If there is a strong desire for the collaborative relationship to be maintained then differences of opinion *will* occur from time to time, but these need not lead to the breakdown of diplomatic relations! 'Normally, we will seek to debate any complaints and deal with any possible financial claims at our regular monthly meetings.' Such a statement might reflect the custom of an insurance broker and, although the presentation of the case might be quite 'robust' at times, both sides know that this is quite healthy.

So, are there any occasions when it is best *not* to negotiate? If one of the parties is quite content with the status quo and there seems to be no advantage to changing they might indulge in considerable 'foot dragging' to avoid debating the point – or even acknowledging its existence. The problem with this approach is that, ultimately, the pressure for change can be irresistible – and quite painful when properly addressed. An industrial relations case may help to make the point.

CASE HISTORY

Trade unions representing employees in the printing industry resisted the adoption of new technology and associated working practices in newspaper companies. The tide of change had been resisted for decades and, when it came, it had almost revolutionary consequences leading to many redundancies. Would it have been less painful if change had been negotiated gradually?

The tide of change cannot be resisted indefinitely!

NEGOTIATING THE BETTER DEAL?

So what can be said about our title? Skilled negotiators – as a matter of course – seek the best possible deals they can and develop a reputation for having high aspirations in their work. Just as important, they try to ensure that their arrangements do not fall apart during the implementation stage (it is one thing to make a deal – it is quite another to make sure that it works).

This is not as easy as it sounds because we are paid to look after the interests of our employing organization – and this is often taken to mean that we should not worry too much about our opponent's satisfaction with a bargain – only whether we have achieved *our* objectives!

In reality, objectives on each side need to interlock and this will be best achieved where agreement is truly mutual. From such a condition, lasting benefits and relationships are gained and the overall value of the agreement is enhanced.

This book is all about the achievement of higher-value agreements through collaborative bargaining and the application of higher-level persuasion skills to achieve those *better* deals. But 'better' in whose eyes? Yours? Theirs? Their boss's? Your boss's? Your team's? Satisfying everyone could be difficult – unless of course you have high aspirations as an achiever. More about this in chapter 3.

REVIEW ASSIGNMENT

Looking back over this chapter, choose a current negotiation case in your own area of responsibility. Ask yourself the following questions:

❏   What is likely to be the predominant culture of the meeting? And why?
(Remember: competitive, consensual, collaborative)

❏   What kind of negotiation opportunity is this?
(Remember: fiscal, occupational, instinctive)

❏ What are the different results I might expect from the negotiation?
(Remember: win/lose, lose/lose, lose/win, win/win)

❏ How could I ensure greater chances of achieving a win/win outcome?

❏ What could be the possible outcomes from *not* negotiating?
(Remember the growing forces for change. If you held them back, what consequences could follow?)

Perceptions of what is, and what is not, negotiation may help establish common ground between negotiators but achieving good results is dependent on the acquisition and use of the core skills.

Chapter 3 provides a full-scale skills audit from which the reader will be able to draw up a personal development plan.

3 The skills audit

INTRODUCTION

As with so many other areas of life, *results* from negotiation will improve when the negotiators have made a conscious effort to develop their skills.

This chapter provides an approach to auditing and targeting the qualities and skills which are used by effective negotiators and the reader will have the opportunity to carry out some self-assessment and target areas for improvement. Two audits are provided:

■ **The practical skills and qualities** (third section)
■ **The skills for advanced levels** (fourth section)

However, for real effectiveness, the reader needs to consider the two learning approaches mentioned in chapter 1:

■ **A firm desire to achieve better – and lasting – negotiated settlements** (the assignments are designed to help with this)
■ **An objective analysis of existing skills – observed by a colleague and/or reviewed through a video recording of an exercise** (providing inescapable evidence of skills and impact on the other parties).

This chapter should be viewed as setting a self-improvement agenda which will be amplified by the following chapters which explore important aspects of negotiation and which will make all the difference when trying to improve results.

BUILDING RELATIONSHIPS

Chapter 2 referred to our abilities in building relationships with other people. It could be argued that, to a large extent, this is dependent on the situations involved. Consider the following:

ASSIGNMENT

❑ A keen football supporter wanting to gain entry to the FA Cup Final may be persuaded to pay a substantial premium price to buy a 'recycled ticket' outside the ground – and may feel totally 'ripped-off' if his or her team then loses!

What motivated him to buy?

❑ A queue of tourists waiting to enter a museum – on a very hot day – may be persuaded to pay an extortionate price for a bottle of water brought to them by a street vendor.

What motivated this purchase?

❑ A supplier reaches agreement with a buyer for the supply of a consumer product – at a very keen price *and is prepared to invest money to help the buyer's business with its marketing.*

What motivated this decision?

'One-off' v. continuing relationships

It isn't just in business that people have to judge the importance of the continuing relationship as opposed to the 'one-night-stand'. The risk of making a mistake when considering the purchase of a car or a house can make some people very reluctant to negotiate or commit themselves to a deal at all. (This may account for many people's dependence on various agents whose role may partly include hand-holding and confidence-building). The 'one-off' deal defeats any need for a continuing relationship (which may ensure some control over the greed motive) and this is a good reason for being cautious in non-repeating deals.

So, it seems sensible to set out with an intention to aim for win/win bargains whenever we negotiate; but how does this fit with the negotiator's personal style and values?

How would you feel if your 'opponent' made a potentially costly error in a meeting and you noticed it – but they did not? Would you:

(a) Immediately point out the error and give your partner the chance to correct it?
(b) Keep quiet and hope it is not spotted until after the delivery takes place?
(c) Distract your opponent – making it less likely the error will be spotted?
(d) Seek to double the order while the error is not spotted?

The desirable answer is obvious – and, if it is not, you might like to consider how you might feel if you were the person who made the unnoticed mistake?

For example, there may be occasions when a supplier needs to move some old stock from the warehouse and fears that it might not be bought at all if he reveals exactly how old it is and just how much of it he has in stock. A good price reduction may be all that is needed for a buyer – who has never dealt with his wholesale business before – to place a substantial order to fill out his stock for the sale.

Culture and styles re-visited

The problem is that many people have double standards – what we quickly *say* and what we actually *do* may be very different – and this can lead to difficulties later. After all, both parties have needs to be met – otherwise there would be no need for the meeting to be held at all. So, how might *your* opponents describe *you*? Competitive, consensual or collaborative? Do you have the flexible ability to vary your approach to meet different scenarios – and how consistent might this feel to the opponent who provides opportunities for all three styles in the one meeting?

(This could involve: being competitive about a proposed price increase this month, being consensual about a consumer survey of attitudes to the products to be carried out by the supplier but with the buyer's clients, and being collaborative over the planned introduction of a new bespoke design service to be offered to clients.)

The best results will be gained from a consistent approach – with predictability in the relationship and trust further developed!

So, an analysis of the motives which lie behind a possible deal needs to be undertaken but, as mentioned in the last chapter, the collaborative (win/win) style is really the best and most secure way of doing business – provided both negotiators have a similar understanding.

THE PRACTICAL SKILLS AND QUALITIES

Here is a set of factors which are known to contribute to effective results in negotiation. After these descriptions, you have the opportunity to rate yourself against the criteria.

Planning

There is little doubt that good planning and preparation contribute substantially to better deals. The trouble is, negotiation tends to encourage a 'macho' effect – especially if we are successful! Characteristically, there can be quite a lot of self-hype about negotiating a deal and, when it is complete, both players can rightfully feel a strong sense of success. The problems can arise when success leads to over confidence and this convinces the negotiator that his or her skills are such that time really does not need to be 'wasted' on planning. (We will explore approaches to planning and research further in chapter 4.)

Aspirations

Skilled negotiators tend to set themselves higher targets to achieve than average negotiators. They become quickly bored with mundane deals and are always looking for ways of enhancing their skills and their results. This approach should not be confused with competitive behaviour – the skilled negotiator is always looking for ways of 'shuffling the cards' to enhance the outcomes considerably.

CASE HISTORY

A leading software supplier in the USA took legal action against a very small competitor because one of their products appeared to breach the copyright laws. After a period of preparation and investigation, the chief executive of the larger company was so impressed by the inventiveness of the staff of the small firm that, instead of risking putting them out of business through the court case, he invested money in their business to around 49 per cent of the equity and gained the benefit of all their creativity and enterprise. The staff of the smaller firm gained from the added security of the relationship and financial backing of the larger group.

High aspirations usually lead to much better deals!

Thinking clearly under stress

When the two sides are locked in deep discussion and either side is manoeuvring to gain the advantage of the debate, thinking clearly is an important skill. The problem is that this often needs to be carried out *while the discussion is proceeding*. How able are you at doing these two things at once – thinking and talking? Less-skilled negotiators either find it difficult to think while speaking and give too much away (or freeze up, and give nothing away risking complete frustration in the opponent) or give too much attention to the thinking process and talk gibberish or waffle!

The other difficulty that some people experience is handling emotional situations. Are *you* affected by the emotions of other parties? Are you easily provoked into an unrestrained response? Does this lead to a worse situation?

CASE HISTORY

A major blue-chip company employed a unit manager who, sadly, suffered from a serious heart complaint, the symptoms of which included a rather short temper. This was well known to the local union organizer who provoked him in meetings to

> the point where he would lose his temper and therefore his
> case. The company transferred him to other duties.
> **Cogent debate is only possible with *self control* and *clear
> thinking*!**

Communicating skills

We often take communications for granted – except when they go
wrong! There are four elements, each of which contribute to
effective communication:

(a)   Vocabulary.
(b)   Speaking and listening.
(c)   Hearing and understanding.
(d)   Non-verbal communications.

(a) Vocabulary

Our basic education gave us a fundamental grasp of our language
and some of this vocabulary we use in everyday situations. However, a negotiator seeks to persuade the other party of the strength of
the case – and the only way in which this can be achieved is through
the language and words used. A good example of this skill is
practised by top lawyers – and, if we were unfortunate enough to
have to employ a QC as defence counsel we would expect the
individual to be able to persuade the court of our innocence through
a persuasive vocabulary.

So, a good vocabulary – and the ability to use the most appropriate word in a particular situation – is an important attribute for a
skilled negotiator.

(b) Speaking and listening

Our abilities to communicate are dependent on the use of an
appropriate communicating style.

In particular, we should be aware of the importance of maintaining a balance between the two elements – speaking/listening. A high
rate of speaking may not always be the most appropriate influencing
style to adopt. However, it is often the trait of a salesperson and this
can also be an individual characteristic which is valuable to a

person's occupation (in fact a sales representative without an extrovert personality might not last very long in the job).

The problems are most likely to occur when one person tries to dominate the conversation with voluble input – giving the other person little chance to contribute. This might appear common sense but it can be a major cause of frustration – and frustrated negotiators often find themselves making very few concessions and might even break off negotiations altogether.

Plain speaking is also a valuable quality as jargon, abbreviations and unusual words may only help to confuse the issues.

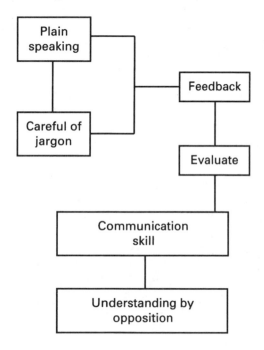

Another kind of difficulty can arise when both negotiators use the extrovert style; they now find themselves competing for 'airspace' and this kind of competition can quickly lead to other competitive win/lose behaviours.

We make an unsafe assumption if we presume that, 'because I am speaking – you are listening', which is why questions can be so valuable in a negotiation meeting (having formed a question and then posed it, it would be a complete waste if we did not listen to the reply).

(c) Hearing and understanding

Listening and hearing are not quite the same thing! We can find ourselves listening to the news but also quite unable to recount the details afterwards – simply because we were busy *thinking about something else at the time*. So, for full comprehension, the listener needs to concentrate hard on both what is said – and what is *not* said! Negotiation without comprehension is highly dangerous and can result in bad deals.

Few of us who have attended committee meetings have not found ourselves 'tuning-out' from the conversation at some point – and have then been amazed at some of the points recorded in the subsequent minutes. How did they get there? Haven't you wondered who really writes the minutes? Failure to listen properly, agreeing (tacitly) to the discussion and then being expected to accept the paperwork, are not recommended behaviours for effective negotiators!

(d) Non-verbal behaviour

There is no doubt that we do communicate with our bodies. Non-verbal communication has become a major topic of conversation since, with careful observation and analysis, it is possible to interpret some of the inner thoughts of opponents.

The problem with body language is that it can be misread. Your opponent is sitting upright, with arms folded and with a rather negative expression. Should you infer from this that he or she is a *reluctant participant* in your meeting, feeling very defensive about what he *thinks* you might say, and shutting out any *proposals* you might have?

All this might be true but your opponent might also be reacting to the cold room, an emotional row with the boss, the car crash on the way over, the puddle he or she stepped in when getting out of the car in the car park. Wouldn't you feel defensive too, in such circumstances?

So, without creating inhibitions for every reader, it has to be said that most skilled negotiators control their body language – but also keep a close eye on any signals they may be able to 'read' from their opponents. There is, however, another way of looking at the use of body language.

Uninhibited behaviour is the province of young children and this is one of the factors which contribute to their charm. In adulthood some people have this wonderful quality known as charisma and, somehow, their uninhibited body language reinforces that quality. So, charismatic negotiators have in-built advantages over the rest of us. Their charm gives them a persuasive power which may enable them to achieve results without the more logical methods described in this book. Put the two together and we are describing a great recipe for even better deals.

Power

Power is a vital factor which cannot be overlooked in negotiation. But this does not necessarily mean the sort of power which is flaunted by one negotiator *over* another – in a competitive atmosphere (risking the start of a win/lose tit-for-tat relationship). Power can also be exercised because one party has something which the other party badly needs – and the scale of need will be best concealed from the meeting. If the parties are working in a collaborative way, power can also be used for the joint benefit of both of them. For example, a major supply agreement could be breaking new ground for both organizations and therefore is probably newsworthy. With the joint names of supplier and customer attached to the deal, there could be considerable column inches to be gained from the overall agreement. Power *can* be completely misread in negotiation; it is an important factor which should never be overlooked as part of the planning stage.

Integrity

In chapter 2 we mentioned the importance of trust between the parties involved; building up a position of trust can take considerable time and effort and yet it can also be 'blown away' in a very short time.

Integrity is a quality which is built up as a result of our behaviour and that of the rest of our organization; it is still an important 'card' in a negotiation. When one player assures the other that a quoted figure (or position) is 'the very best I can do' – who is to know that is the truth and that there are no further fallback positions still available?

Relations between the two organizations will be enhanced when everyone who is party to an agreement behaves with integrity (for example, neither side raises false complaints or tries to get the other side to take more responsibility for things going wrong than they are really happy to accept). This may be easier said than done and needs to cover genuine mistakes as well as detailed implementation of the agreement. (How many people telephone their supplier if or when an overage on an order is delivered? Contrast this with the speed with which they may be contacted when there is a short delivery.) Is it any surprise that some things we might say in the negotiation meeting might be taken with a pinch of salt by our opponents? Skilled negotiators use their integrity to build a convincing case.

Open-mindedness

Another important characteristic for negotiators to maintain is open-mindedness. This is more difficult than it sounds – 'Of course I'm open-minded', you might say. The problem is that, in the course of preparing for a negotiation, we tend to narrow choices down to just one or two options – and probably a preferred one of those two schemes. So, when we meet the other party we may find that they have also selected a preferred option – but this is not even on our preferred list.

It is at this point that it is important to recognize that who invented or owns the idea does not really matter – the question is, will it work? Will it achieve the desired objectives? Effective negotiators are sufficiently flexible to be able to respond to each option as it arises – regardless of who invented it!

Decision-making

There is nothing worse than working with an indecisive negotiator or manager. There comes a time in every meeting when a decision has to be taken – and this should not mean simply to convene yet another meeting. Effective negotiators try to ensure that all the necessary facts are available at the meeting and, if they are not, that appropriate recesses are taken to close any gaps.

Failure to reach an agreement can be for a number of reasons – but of most concern is the thought that perhaps one of the negotiators does not have the authority to make the decision. This can undermine an individual's credibility to the point where his or her opponent seeks a way of presenting the case to a more senior person in the other party's organization.

Persistence

Our last category is a major benefit to those of us who are working through difficult economic conditions – or periods of uncertainty. Obtaining a clear agreement from a client or supplier can require a significant amount of persistence and determination and sometimes this may even include the process of obtaining an interview.

Skilled negotiators know that agreement can often be obtained and that an outright 'no' can be turned into a 'well, maybe we could consider ...' and then into a 'this seems to be the best way forward'! There is often a right time for an agreement and gentle pressure and persuasion will often be rewarded – eventually.

Now that we have explored these basic characteristics, let us introduce a short assignment.

ASSIGNMENT 1

The following chart shows the characteristics and a self-assessment chart – please draw a circle around your *present standard* as you see yourself; then mark your desired rating *as you think it should be* with a cross. The result of this should be an identification of 'performance gaps' in the last 13 factors described above.

Factor	*Score*						
Planning	1	2	3	4	5	6	7
Aspirations	1	2	3	4	5	6	7
Thinking	1	2	3	4	5	6	7
Communication	1	2	3	4	5	6	7
Vocabulary	1	2	3	4	5	6	7

Speak/listen	1	2	3	4	5	6	7
Hear/understand	1	2	3	4	5	6	7
Non-verbal	1	2	3	4	5	6	7
Power	1	2	3	4	5	6	7
Integrity	1	2	3	4	5	6	7
Open-mind	1	2	3	4	5	6	7
Decisiveness	1	2	3	4	5	6	7
Persistence	1	2	3	4	5	6	7

ACTION PLAN

Any item which you rated below a 4 *for present skills* really deserves some urgent attention. Try to plan some specific action for these factors:

Factor	*Action proposed*	*Target completion date*

NEGOTIATING SKILLS FOR ADVANCED LEVELS

When having to negotiate at higher levels of authority, or dealing with more skilful opponents, the skills and attributes in this section will help the negotiator achieve better results whilst maintaining the best collaborative style with the other parties involved. Again, we will explore the importance of each factor and, through a skills audit, encourage a personal analysis of strengths and weaknesses.

Leading and controlling discussion

There are benefits to be gained from leading a meeting – whether you are in the chair or not; for one reason, leadership usually provides the opportunity of presenting one's own ideas. However, negotiation is also about *sharing* concepts and options and this is less likely to happen if the presenter is too forceful, dogmatic or fails to offer enough speaking time to the other party.

Control in a negotiation discussion does not necessarily follow from being voluble. There are a number of conversation techniques which provide the user with control – without it being immediately obvious. These include the use of **open questions**, **summaries** and **clarifying behaviours** (see below).

Another factor which affects leadership and control includes the negotiator's natural leaning towards extrovert behaviour. As we have seen, it is quite natural for salespeople to have few inhibitions about making verbal presentations to clients – an extrovert personality will probably have been included as a desirable personality trait in the sales manager's recruitment plan in the first place. However, extrovertness can easily become 'pushiness' and this might well create a natural reaction in opponents. Moreover, an extrovert person may be easily manipulated to give away any number of secrets in a meeting – simply through the desire to be helpful, or to impress the opponent.

Negotiation control begins with self-control!

Forming and using proposals to progress the meeting

Discussion, on its own, cannot progress a meeting without consideration of those original aims and objectives we recorded earlier. After a thorough exploration of the issues, it is normal for one of the two parties to begin to put together some proposals. Initially, these will be tentative: 'Well, supposing we were prepared to ... would you then consider ... ?'

This example also introduces the idea of the **conditional proposal** – i.e. the idea of tentatively offering something to the opponent, but only if the other person offers something to you. Whilst this might seem an obvious point to an experienced negotiator, the skill lies in:

■ preparing objectives and possible concessions – as part of the planning *before* the negotiation meeting;
■ establishing advantageous 'trade-offs' (which means thinking out what concessions the other side may have to offer);
■ presenting proposals in an attractive and persuasive way.

Tentative or trial proposals can be followed up by more concrete suggestions once they have attracted a measure of agreement from the other party and it is important that this level of agreement is carefully tested for failures of listening and comprehension.

Building and supporting

There are few features of meetings more demotivating than the constant attempts of other people to rubbish your ideas. It is therefore much more satisfying to feel that we each contributed to the overall pool of suggestions and proposals which resulted in an eventual deal.

Part of this effect grows from a recognition on behalf of one negotiator that he or she does not have a monopoly of solutions to the issues involved in the meeting, and is sufficiently open-minded to allow for the possibility that neither party will have prepared the *only* way forward. Another aspect of the creation of a motivating atmosphere in the meeting lies in the actual behaviours we use to develop mutual agreement.

Disagreement, whilst important in establishing that there may be points in the conversation which *are not agreed*, can become a somewhat frustrating style habit. It can become extremely annoying to be inventing ideas and proposals to put forward only to have them attacked and demolished by your opponent and, if this continues, there is a good chance that the meeting will be brought to an end prematurely.

A rather more effective style involves the negotiator focusing on the aspects of the other party's proposals which he or she *can* agree with, expressing support for those ideas and *building on* those new points which would make the proposals more acceptable and attractive to him or her.

Seeking information

Successful negotiation often turns on the use of information. It has been said that information is power – and, even if this were only half true, then it would endorse the importance of the planning (and researching) phase. The more information that you can assemble *before* the negotiation meeting, the more likely you will avoid unpleasant surprises and being influenced by 'spur of the moment' revelations.

No matter how thoroughly the planning has been carried out, there will still be some information which can only be confirmed by the other party in your meeting. So, some carefully prepared questions will help to draw out that confirmation – or even *new* information – in these areas.

Most sales training programmes teach the importance of using 'open' questions, i.e. those which begin with:

WHAT? WHEN? WHO? WHERE? HOW? and WHEN?

---

and the technique should be adopted by any negotiator – regardless of their function. The principal benefit shows in the additional control which questions can give.

Most of us were brought up to respect others and to behave politely – to speak when spoken to and to answer when asked a question. This conditioning runs deep with many people who will dutifully break off their current speech pattern to allow their opponent to ask a question – and will then set about answering it. Observers on our Advanced Negotiation Skills workshops quickly identify a swing in behaviour – success in questioning by one party reveals increased information given by the other. This often leads to a competitive edge in the results gained by the questioner.

Giving information

Many of the behaviours used in an average negotiation meeting fall into this category; whilst facts and opinions do need to be shared (there would be little point in holding a meeting if they were not), progress in the negotiation could be hampered by too much waffle and verbiage. The behaviours which enable progress to be made are *proposals* and, if too much information or opinion is given, progress towards agreement can be impaired and serious frustration can result.

Bringing-in

In everyday conversation we practise the art of listening to each other; in fact the mark of good conversationalists is that the interaction flows naturally from topic to topic and real interest seems to be generated in each party's contribution. We use quite subtle methods to control the effects of domination by one of the parties – or to change the topics if we become less interested in the main one.

Initially, we express a loss of interest – or a desire to interrupt – by breaking eye contact. If this goes unnoticed by the other person we may repeat it or actually look away. If this is still ineffective we might raise one hand slightly in a 'please desist' gesture – and if this does not work we might open the mouth as if about to speak. As a last resort, we might actually *talk over* the other party and so try to break in!

Mostly, none of these activities should be necessary if the other person sees the need and opportunity to bring the other person into the conversation.

Timing

A negotiator does need a good sense of timing if his or her impact is to be optimized. For example, there are good and bad times for:

- introducing new ideas;
- taking a recess;
- summarizing;
- closing the meeting.

There are also good and bad times to invite a negotiation . . . and times when it is best to negotiate alone and when it is best to be accompanied.

Assertiveness

Much has been written about this subject in recent years and it is certainly a skill which is valuable in negotiation situations. Non-assertive behaviour in negotiation may be waffly, apologetic and weak; the speaker may even speak with one hand in front of his or her mouth and avoid eye contact – as if trying to shirk responsibility for what is being said. Non-assertion invites disagreement, outright rejection or even hectoring – and provides little future for a truly collaborative settlement.

In contrast, aggression provides little respect for the values or rights of the other people and, if results are achieved, it is often through a sheer misuse of power. Non-assertive negotiators might attract the 'sympathy vote' occasionally – but rarely achieve consistent results. Aggressive people often acquire acquiescence (and enemies!) and rarely any special favours.

When the chips are down, every negotiator needs a favour or two!

Testing understanding and summarizing

These are clarifying behaviours and, when the pressure is on in a meeting, they can be exceptionally helpful. How many times have you been involved in a meeting and not been 100 per cent sure of what has been discussed or agreed? This could be highly dangerous and skilled negotiators will often make notes at the meeting and seek to exchange them with their opponent to indicate confirmation of the agreement. This helps to avoid the common syndrome at committee meetings which involves minutes which are written up after the meeting and 'corrected' by the secretary or chair and maybe passed 'on the nod' at the next meeting because no one bothered to check them! Negotiators who fall into this trap nearly always live to regret it! So, there is every reason to use frequent summaries during a negotiation because these are *clarifying behaviours* – reducing the possibilities of oversight or error.

Similarly, a skilled negotiator never allows any chances of misunderstanding to pass by without challenge. This can be easier said than done – especially where the culture leans towards abbreviations or technical jargon. (Hans Christian Andersen's fable about the Emperor's new clothes applies here – technical jargon should always be challenged!)

BEHAVIOURS BEST AVOIDED

Skilled negotiators should always try to *avoid* the following behaviours:

Defence/attack spirals – these are provoked disagreements which are deliberately emotionally charged. The purpose is to distract the opponent from the main agenda point and can result in uncontrolled conflict. The point is that the issues raised are rarely solved and any straight talking may simply divide the parties rather than encourage a meeting of minds.

CASE HISTORY: NUM/COAL BOARD

In the infamous coal strike of 1973, the media gave a great deal of attention to any sign of negotiation activity between the two sides. In the absence of any factual data about what actually happened in private meetings, conclusions are often drawn from what is disclosed outside the room. After one particular 'progress meeting' between the Chairman of the Coal Board and the President of the NUM (which lasted approximately one and a half minutes!), the latter complained that there was little point in taking part in a meeting when one's opponent 'has a bag over his head'. This expression fascinated journalists who dutifully reported the comment.

What did he mean? Was it a literal comment – or did it reveal that, in his view, his opponent was not able to listen (or was not interested)? Was this a response to 'megaphone' negotiating tactics implying that an alternative approach was desired by the opponent – or was it a reaction designed simply to 'wind up' the trade union leader? However the point might be interpreted, this particular meeting made no contribution to ending what was, ultimately, an extremely expensive stoppage all round!

Defence and attack behaviours are rarely used by effective negotiators.

Disagreeing is inevitable in negotiation, especially where the two parties are starting from opposite positions. However, skilled negotiators try to emphasize common ground rather than the issues which divide them – with the intention of gradually building closer (not wider-apart) relationships.

CASE HISTORY: ISRAELIS/PALESTINIANS

In the now famous peace talks which were brokered by the Norwegians, one prominent Palestinian, described just how fruitless it eventually became attending daily meetings at which he was expected to read out the same prepared statement. After ten or more weeks of this he began to wonder whether there was not a better use of his time, and this realization led him to consider how the impasse might be broken. At the next formal meeting he shared his feelings with the full assembly and this broke the deadlock. The rest is history!

Reasoned disagreement is always preferable to conflict.

Counter-proposals are usually the mark of a competitive negotiation. 'Black and white' issues are typically involved where one person's 'win' represents the other party's 'loss'; for example, straightforward haggling results in price negotiation in such small movements that the whole process becomes really tedious and frustrating – which can lead to a stand-off in the meeting schedule.

Shutting out your opponent is often a symptom of competitive negotiation. It involves over-talking the other person and is really rude – apart from irritating! On a practical front, such behaviour usually means that neither party is capable of listening to the other – so there is little point in continuing. Whilst the rational logic of *not* doing this is strong, different cultures may not see it the same way. For example, some countries close to the Mediterranean seem to encourage debates that are both 'free ranging' and noisy. Groups of people will join the conversation until several people are competing for a hearing – thus destroying any chance of meaningful communication. This can be great fun but it may not produce any progress.

Blocking is a conversational tactic which can cause intense frustration. Literally it is a method of 'placing a block' in the path of the negotiation and is stronger in effect than simple disagreement as no reason is usually given. Expressions such as 'We couldn't agree to that' or 'That's no good to me' can create real irritation in the opponent as a reason could be discussed and probably made more flexible. Skilled negotiators do not use blocking tactics.

NEGOTIATING THE BETTER DEAL

ASSIGNMENT 2: THE SKILLS AUDIT AT ADVANCED LEVELS

Now that we have reviewed the more advanced skills, here is another chance to identify those which you feel may need some enhancement.

Factor	Score						
	1	*2*	*3*	*4*	*5*	*6*	*7*
Lead/control							
Proposing							
Building/supporting							
Seeking information							
Giving information							
Bringing-in							
Timing							
Assertiveness							
Testing understanding/ summarizing							
Defence/attack							

Disagreeing							
Counter proposals							
Shutting out							
Blocking							

ACTION PLAN

Any item which you rated below a '4' for present skills really deserves some urgent attention. Try to plan some specific goals and action for these factors – perhaps some observation input and practical project work.

Factor	Action proposed	Target completion date

Now that you have some skills targets to achieve, you should find the following chapters more valuable in your quest for better deals. Chapter 4 introduces a structured approach to negotiation and then reveals how skilled negotiators often discard this approach!

4 *Introducing PROD-ProSC*

INTRODUCTION

Most tasks become easier and less intimidating when we have some guidelines to apply. This could be said to be true of cooking, changing the oil in the car or preparing the departmental budget – and negotiation is no different.

This chapter proposes a structured approach to the task of negotiation – and then discards it! Why? Because, whilst skilled negotiators will apply a systematic approach to their *preparation*, the actual implementation may appear to be much more flexible – and will therefore allow greater scope for the use of their skills, personality and possible charisma. However, it is important that the style of the meeting does not overtake the progress and achievements to be gained by both sides – an issue which we will resurrect towards the end of the chapter.

Our mnemonic – PROD-ProSC – provides a framework for the systematic process we have built this chapter around. It stands for:

P   = Preparation (incorporating people and places)
R   = Research
O   = Opening
D   = Discussion
Pro   = Proposals
S   = Summarizing
C   = Close

PREPARATION – PEOPLE AND PLACES

People – likes and dislikes

There is no doubt that people can be an important tactical resource in negotiation. Assignment 1 in chapter 2 will have graphically illustrated this point!

We might all try to present the most likeable qualities in our personality to people we are trying to influence – and this will certainly make an effective contribution towards our negotiation goals. However, we also need to remember that our opponents are subjective human beings (just like us!) and they have their likes and dislikes about other people which can obscure or obstruct progress towards objectives. So, the first point to remember is that known inhibitions in the make-up of your opponent should be:

- researched
- planned for
- dealt-with

in such a way as to minimize any negative effects. This could include recasting negotiator roles if, for example, you discover that your opponent would prefer to deal with a woman or, perhaps, a man. It could also be that they are more respectful of an opponent with some grey hair rather than an obvious 'whiz-kid!' – or maybe the reverse!

Within the constraints of hierarchy, it is generally best to 'field' the most persuasive negotiator – especially when there are known preferences. This advice might not match with our preferences for an equal and egalitarian society but that should be a separate agenda item for a different set of meetings elsewhere! Negotiators should not confuse their agenda objectives in such meetings.

CASE HISTORY

Two young female sales negotiators were discussing the week's appointments in a hotel lobby. On discovering that her first call the next day had previously been visited by her colleague, the first representative was heard to ask: 'Is he [the client] the type of man who would appreciate a mini-skirt or would you recommend I wear a maxi with the open side-seam?'

However much such plans and tactics might be deprecated, it has to be remembered that some 'opponents' may be influenced by them.

For many years the City of London worked on the principle that the 'uniform' of a pin-striped suit conveyed a traditional culture –

and this formed an element of comfort about negotiators. Such standards may be puzzling to readers who have not experienced the dress codes used in such a close industry but, when new deals are being struck between negotiators who have not met before, dress codes and appearance can provide important hurdles for the participants to overcome.

Failure to pay attention to the expectations of the other party can result in the loss of an important deal!

Self-presentation

Some people play on their appearance or presentation style in order to intimidate their opponents. For example, a large person can sometimes present him or herself in an aggressive way in the sure knowledge that the departmental team (or union membership?) will not argue with such intimidation. This effect can be gained from:

■ physical size – emphasized by unrestrained gestures(!);
■ a loud voice;
■ a hectoring manner;
■ a 'larger-than-life' personality.

CASE HISTORY

Mr Khrushchev, diminutive one-time leader of the USSR during the height of the East–West Cold War, created an amazing effect on the world by an unrestrained response to a debate at the United Nations. Interrupting a particularly significant debate, he sent shock waves around the world by removing one of his shoes and banging it aggressively on the table before him as he shouted 'Niet, Niet, Niet'!

Similar dramatic effects were perpetrated by Dom Mintoff in his negotiations with the British over the future of the Royal Naval base in Malta. He was known to lose his temper when a meeting did not go his way, stand on his chair and shake his fist at his opponents – using the full psychological advantage of the extra height.

Histrionics should always be treated coolly in negotiation meetings!

Bullying of this kind *can* be effective in negotiating meetings – especially where the opponent has little alternative but to deal with the person who perpetrates the 'bullying'. Such use or misuse of power can be very effective in the *short term* – but can also generate determined opposition in the longer term! We will return to this tactical effect in a later chapter.

Ask yourself: consider your influencing skills and 'presence'.
Have you consciously analysed your:

❏ Personal presentation – e.g. power dressing, colour coding etc.

❏ Manner of speech – e.g. power of vocabulary, pronunciation, accent etc.

❏ Charm/charisma – e.g. the way in which you are able present the pleasing side of your personality

❏ Presentation skills – e.g. your ability to speak easily and clearly with people at all levels, to maintain an appropriate pace and to communicate clearly.

❏ Body language – e.g. the way in which you are able to use your own body language to influence your opponent – 'laid back' or 'pushy'?

ASSIGNMENT 1

Rate yourself on the following chart and then ask someone who knows you well to undertake the same task and then compare notes; alternatively, a video workshop may reveal some interesting improvement areas.

Attributes	Your perspective Score 1–9	Colleague's perspective Score 1–9
Personal presentation		
Manner of speech		
Charm/charisma		
Presentation skills		
Body language		

Scores: 1 = without positive influence (may even create negative influence!)

9 = very influential, positive influence.

Place

To the rational person, the thought that the venue for a negotiating meeting might affect its outcome may seem totally absurd. However, most people have strong likes and dislikes – although some of these may not be conscious ones – and personal physical or psychological comfort can affect a meeting greatly.

Consider the options. Do you prefer to negotiate 'at home' or 'away'? Either option provides strengths and weaknesses – opportunities and threats. Many managers would consider that meeting on home territory means that they have the opportunity to 'manage' the meeting – in terms of the physical factors (e.g. interruptions, distractions, tidiness of surroundings etc.) and that provision of coffee, food etc. can help to make the meeting go well.

On the other hand, marketers will often draw attention to the great advantage it can be 'playing away' because of the additional learning opportunities provided by observation of the condition of the building (and vehicles outside!), the demeaning way in which an apparently senior executive may be hectored (in interruptions of what was supposed to be a private meeting) and apparent inability to cope with excesses of paper!

Much of this might seem unimportant – and to skilled negotiators it can be. However, confidence in these meetings is important and the slightest 'discomfort' *can* make a difference when the pressure is on. For example, a meeting being held in the middle of a retail selling department – where samples are being considered by a buyer while retail customers are browsing nearby – may intimidate either buyer *or* seller because cost prices and margins may be discussed and these need to be kept from the customers nearby. (The question has to be asked – which of the 'players' is more likely to be discomforted?)

CASE HISTORY: CHILD CUSTODY CASES

Solicitors report that the place of a negotiation can speed along decisions in emotive cases such as those involving child custody. Parents or guardians who find it easy to block all proposals before going to court – from the comfort and security of a civilized, centrally heated, solicitor's office – can suddenly find themselves confronted with hastily convened discussions over the custody of their children forced upon them by the court – and only a draughty corridor as a venue. This can be a daunting experience – especially when the emotions are involved, in full public view.

The venue of the negotiation *can* bring important tactical advantages in itself!

RESEARCH

Better deals are undoubtedly achievable and the level of effort devoted to research and preparation can make a big difference. A negotiator who has prepared the case thoroughly and *knows what has been agreed elsewhere*, will have a distinct advantage over average negotiators who do not have this knowledge. It is not just that this knowledge brings more confidence – it is also that more pressure can be applied in strength of argument to secure a more advantageous deal!

So, for better deals, the negotiator should expect to put more effort into research!

How can this be done? In the modern world, there are few secrets. Most organizations take steps to ensure that key decisions or strategies are coded 'Company Confidential' and, by implication, are prepared to impose the ultimate sanction against anyone who reveals all. This may not stop leaks, however. Any time that employees leave the organization, knowledge goes with them, and this is how many people enhance their market worth in the first place. So, an important and sizeable deal may be influenced considerably by nuggets of information which are obtainable from a former employee or a dissatisfied one.

If this hint at 'guerrilla' tactics offends the reader, it should not. Attempts may be being made – at this very moment – to root out your organization's marketing strategy or five-year business plans by some aggressive competitor!

Apart from the disaffected employee, a great deal of useful information about *current* trading conditions can often be obtained from casual conversations with present, possibly lower-level, employees. Such worthies may not have been briefed on how to behave with outsiders and may be a valuable source of 'native intelligence'. It is amazing how helpful cleaners, drivers, receptionists, post workers and service technicians can be!

Quite aside from this kind of investigation, skilled negotiators will ensure that they are armed with the most up-to-date facts about the marketplace in which they are working and this is where the specialist can score above the occasional operator. For example, an estate agent's advice is valuable if it is possible to obtain factual information about the recent valuations of property similar to yours – and, more importantly, the realized sale values. Seeing many customers pass through the showroom, enables the agent to evaluate the current market in a way which may be difficult – if not impossible – by the average vendor. Certainly it would take considerable effort and time.

In this respect, buyers and sellers who are in the fast-moving consumer goods markets have a currency which is extremely valuable to competitors operating in the same marketplace; once a negotiator is out of touch for any length of time (e.g. through redundancy), past experience may have become out of date and considerable research may be needed to succeed with a re-entry into the market. Such knowledge of the going rate for current deals is extremely valuable in the negotiation process – making win/win deals easier and quicker to achieve.

KEY FORMAT

If you are about to prepare for a negotiation, the following checklist will help you establish the areas of research which may be needed:

Recent agreements

■ What recent agreements might be used to 'benchmark' this proposal?

....

....

Sources of information

■ How/where can I find out more about these agreements? What is known in the public domain? (E.g. press, research panels, people involved etc.)

....

....

Key 'influences'

■ Who are the 'influencers' in this field? Who may be influencing your opponents (and general level of expectations in this field)? What are they saying about the position *you* are facing?

....

....

■ What plans do the parties have for the future (e.g. new models/products, job restructuring, new recruitment or training plans) which might affect the value of the product or service affected by the current deal?

....

....

OPENING

At first sight it may seem superfluous to discuss how to open a meeting here, but the tone for what might follow is often set by things said or *not said* in the early stages. Carefully managed *openings* can help negotiators to:

■ assess the strength of character and personality(ies) of the other person or team;
■ judge the mood of the others;
■ understand a little of their background, interests and motivation;
■ learn about current organizational preoccupations, objectives and even crises!

Personality

A typical business greeting in the UK involves a handshake and this can transmit quite a lot of information about those meeting – especially that person's social skills and personality. Grades of handshake can vary from the power-crazed 'crusher' to the 'wet fish' shake. Much has been read into these extremes (not to mention the additional factors of whose hand is in the dominant position – or what it might mean when the other person also clasps your elbow with their spare hand!) but certainly these factors do tell us something about the other person's awareness of their effect on other people.

This aspect should not be confused with good manners the absence of which also may tell us a great deal about the other person – but this may not make the individual any better or worse a negotiator! For further consideration of these aspects the reader could do little better than to read Dale Carnegie's classic book *How to Win Friends and Influence People*!

Mood

The moment you enter the host's office you may assess the mood of your opponent which could give a fair indication of how the meeting may progress. Highly skilled influencers see these early stages as providing good opportunities to establish the meeting on a positive footing from the start. This may be through careful 'pacing' of the other person's speech patterns and mirroring their body language. Some measure of good old-fashioned charm may also help the meeting along.

Even so, the other party may give off strongly negative or cold feelings and it is easy to assume that these are directed at you or your organization. However, this may not be the case. For example, the person you are meeting may have had a simply dreadful morning – fell over the cat on the way down the stairs, crashed the car on the way to the station, missed the train and been late for work, and then discovered that the departmental budget has been sliced in half without any consultation! After such a chapter of bad news anyone could be excused for being a little icy. So, if you are visiting with the intention of re-establishing a service contract which has lapsed and resulted in some rather high and unexpected bills for your client, you may well assume the worst (that the cold atmosphere is solely directed at *you* and you are on a loser from the start). It should also be remembered that some negotiators use these cold tactics to unsettle their opponent at the start of a meeting – and, if this tactic is suspected, the visitor needs to have a strategy for handling the situation.

Background, interests, motivation

Many mistakes have been made in meetings through negotiators rushing into a business discussion without exploring the possible common ground they share with their opponent. The Japanese have much to teach us in this field. When your contract and relationship may last initially for two to three years (and potentially for a lot longer) it is very important that we have a clear understanding of each other. This might well extend into consideration of professional background, family life, hobbies and career aims – and especially giving insights into culture, values and integrity. In other words, the parties are piecing together a full picture of their opponent's background and the degree to which they might be trusted.

The key point to remember here is that common ground can be exceptionally valuable when external events conspire to divide you and your organization!

Organization preoccupations and objectives

General discussion at the start of a meeting gives the participants the opportunity to explore the current aims, success stories and possible challenges being experienced in their business life. This tuning-in process can be extremely valuable as genuine information may be revealed about the business which could be of great interest in the subsequent discussion on the business agenda. This phase also provides the negotiators with the opportunity to set the scene with information about their organization's needs or philosophy. The key point to remember here is that:

All players need to be able to 'sell' their organization's needs in a negotiation.

Good selling skills should not be seen as the sole province of the salesperson!

DISCUSSION

After the ice-breaking phase of the meeting it should move naturally into the early stages of discussion. This progressive step will be affected by, amongst other things, the time either party has allocated to the meeting. In fact this information is often a key factor in influencing what can be achieved in the meeting. In these days of concern with individual productivity, time and stress management, all parties will have priorities to meet and today's meeting should be seen as just one episode in the parties' lives. Put into this kind of context it is easier to understand how things can go wrong. For example;

■ the start of one meeting is delayed by the late-running of the previous meeting;
■ objectives are affected by other negotiations, which have yet to be resolved;
■ interruptions occur through progress or obstacles being encountered in arrangements with related schemes, deals or suppliers/clients.

In each case such difficulties may be ascribed to the inefficiencies of the appropriate negotiator – or perhaps the disorganization of the business – but the fast-moving nature of the marketplace may make the scenario endemic to business arrangements in the sector. So, it is important for the players to set some goals for the meeting alongside an understanding of the quantity of time which can be made available.

If a significant difference between skilled and average negotiators lies in the effort they put into preparing for the negotiation, the perception, incisive grasp of the issues and persuasive style of discussion used by the negotiator can make all the difference to the effectiveness of the early stages of the meeting.

PROPOSE

Inexperienced negotiators often have difficulty in progressing a meeting from the maze of discussion towards the finishing-line of a deal. They find it difficult to piece together the issues and are uncertain on how to gain their objectives without giving anything away. The solution rests in this vital stage – the presentation and use of proposals which provide the only way in which the negotiation meeting can move forward. There are two kinds of proposal: trial proposals and conditional proposals.

Trial proposals

These provide the best route forward for tentative negotiators; the reason for the delineation trial is that the proposals offered in this way are attempts to find out if the other party is ready (or can be persuaded) to move forward. Here is an example of the kind of phraseology which might be used at this stage:

■ Well, suppose *we* were able to . . . , would *you* consider it a possibility to . . . ?' Because the proposal is tentative, it allows for the possibility that it could be rejected – or perhaps worse – accepted far too readily! There would still be a chance of revising the proposal by either side if it is unacceptable or, perhaps, thought to be over- or under-generous.

Proposals

Proposals become more concrete as they are pieced together in the meeting and as the agenda is progressed. The most important technique used by skilled negotiators is the formation of *conditional proposals*. This means indicating that the proposals are conditional on the other party's action – for example:

■ *'If* you are prepared to order the product in boxes of ten *and* accept our minimum quantities, *then* we would accept your price proposal.'

The vital point here is that the cheaper price *is* available to the other party *provided* the conditions are met. That is . . . *something for something (quid pro quo!).*

Naïve negotiators may become confused at this stage and find themselves using another (mistaken) form of proposal:

■ If we could offer these larger orders then we could also put them on display in our new branches we have just taken over.'

This is obviously not *quid pro quo* – and could lead to very bad deals indeed!

SUMMARIZE

As we will see later, the contribution of summaries in a meeting can offer significant advantages to all those present. Without a summary, discussion can revolve around the issues several times with either player simply repeating subjects and topics already covered in some detail. Apart from the fact that this may appear boring and repetitive (and therefore demotivate the participants) the discussion may not contribute clarity to the meeting – quite the reverse in fact!

So, apart from raising the spectre of misunderstanding and confusion, the absence of strategic summaries may contribute to considerable errors in the ultimate agreement – and possibly the contract or communiqué! How many times have we heard it said:

■ 'But I thought we/they agreed . . .'?
■ 'I was sure that we agreed that, but it does not seem to be in the minutes'?
■ 'You did include cancellation terms in the contract, didn't you?'

In reality, negotiators cannot spend too much time in summarizing behaviour and, if used effectively, good summaries will help the meeting towards its final phase.

CLOSE

In a negotiation meeting, there will usually be a result. Unlike other kinds of meetings, whose purpose may be to inform, update, evaluate etc., the parties to a negotiation normally have specific goals to achieve; progress towards these objectives may indicate the appropriateness of a closing point in the meeting.

At this point perhaps we should review our original purpose in meetings; there may have been clear requirements for us to achieve a win/win, win/lose, or even a lose/lose result, and summaries will give either party the chance to consider whether *sufficient progress* has been made to enable a final agreement to be made. If this is not possible, the parties may agree simply to meet again in the future (diarized or not!). The lack of any positive intention arising from the meeting may indicate:

- a lack of intention or motivation in the first instance;
- the leaching away of good intentions, before the meeting started, for some reason discussed or experienced in the meeting itself;
- a recognition that the issues are more complicated/technical/vague/detailed than could be realistically tackled in the time allowed for the meeting.

It is often the mark of inexperienced negotiators that the most they feel able to agree is the date of a further meeting! This is not to say that either party should feel *obliged* to agree when they are unsure about the sense of doing this. Clearly, most negotiations take place in an environment of *free will* and this means that there may *not* be an agreement from *this* meeting – it is, after all, part of our right to think about it!

We will consider, later, techniques for closing the gap between discussion/proposals and the final decision. Suffice to say here that **skilled negotiators** do not waste time in clarifying any remaining inhibitions or sticking points and closing the deal where possible. This is especially important when the *implementation of the agreement* is considered. After all the earlier discussion of the issues, it may be that loose ends of implementation may turn the deal sour. For example:

- 'Who will be responsible for writing up this agreement?'
- 'Where and when shall we convene for this review meeting?'
- 'How will this delivery be made, and when?'

These may seem obvious points but many negotiations have come to grief through inadequate coverage of the detail – and the details often make the difference between a win/win and a lose/lose deal.

SEQUENCED MEETINGS – OR NOT?

The PROD-ProSC formula provides a valuable framework for us to use in set-piece negotiations, but will it always work? The odd thing about negotiation is that better results are generally obtainable when *the players are equally well trained.* In other words, advantage may be gained by one side or the other but the overall aim should be for a 'quality win' – one which benefits all parties.

By reverse argument, the failure to adopt a sequenced approach to the meeting does not necessarily indicate a naïve or untrained negotiator. It may point to a deliberate attempt to form an individual style – or gain some tactical advantage and, when coupled with the exercise of a charismatic personality, the result can be extraordinarily effective.

So, whilst the logical approach to the meeting may appear to be the best (and only) method to adopt, the reader should always be alert to unstructured approaches and develop the ability to use or respond to these too. After all, chess grand masters spend large periods of their lives trying to out-think the strategies of their opponents – with a very large, personal prize at stake. The enthusiastic negotiator could do worse than to emulate this example.

NEGOTIATING THE BETTER DEAL

This chapter has made the case for thorough preparation before a negotiation takes place. It might be thought by some readers that the amount of time invested in this process is out of balance with the value of the deal – or the issues at stake. If this is the case then, clearly, this particular negotiation task ought to be delegated to a more junior employee – whose time is not so expensive. However, they may need training and briefing before this can be done.

REVIEW ASSIGNMENT

Taking a negotiation situation you have to tackle in the course of the next weeks, try using the PROD-ProSC format as a preparation model. Plan for yourself the sequence you would hope to experience:

Stage	*Issues*
P = Preparation (a) People	Who am I meeting? With what authority? Who else is likely to be present? What do I know about the culture and style of representatives of this business?
(b) Place	Where will we meet? Home or away? What is the meeting room like? How can I make the communications work for me? How affected am I likely to be by the personal-comfort factors?
R = Research	What do we know about the trend of deals in this sector? How might this affect our goals? Have I got a clear shopping list of objectives and parameters worked out for each one? What could be our opponents' position? How could I find out in advance? Who might have the 'power' in this relationship? How could it be used for mutual benefit?
O = Opening	How should I open the meeting? What 'ice-breaking' topics might be used? Are there any probing questions I could use? How could we establish some common ground?
D = Discussion	What style of conversation should I adopt? Collaborative/consensus/competitive? What kind of response is this likely to bring?

Pro = Propose	How will I resist the temptation to move too quickly/slowly? How could trial proposals help? How will I ensure that all *my proposals* are conditional?
S = Summarize	How good am I at using summaries in meetings? How will I remember to use summaries – during and at the end of the meeting?
C = Close	Who will be responsible for tracking progress at the meeting – and at the end? How can I ensure that appropriate notes are taken and that they are accurate and complete? How strong is my decision-making ability? What methods of closing can I use most effectively? How will I manage issues of my own authority – where these may be challenged?

Lastly, you should consider how you will evaluate the negotiation meeting and the deal you arrive at:

The deal itself	*Stages*
How satisfied am I with the final deal?	How effective were my preparations and use of the stages?
How well was I able to use concessions to obtain movement and my objectives?	Which areas might need strengthening next time?

Is this deal a real 'win/win'?	
Learning points	*Action Plan*

Chapter 5 sets us off with a detailed approach of the first stage of the negotiation structure – preparation and research.

5 *Preparation and research*

INTRODUCTION

Skilled negotiators know how large a part planning, preparation and research can play in helping achieve a better deal – and, remember, this 'better deal' measure should be capable of assessment by *both parties* – after the meeting! This chapter focuses on a disciplined approach to preparation and lays out a structured way of bringing all the necessary data together – in a usable format.

There is something strange about the effect which constant or frequent negotiation has on some people. They often become ebullient – self-confident almost to the point of being 'cock-sure' – and egotistic. Their track record of successes may encourage the thought that their successes are more to do with personal character-istics rather than any actions or techniques used in meetings – in fact an aura of a 'macho sport' begins to form around their memoirs of successes achieved in foreign climes or with 'major players' in markets renowned for their difficulties.

Such personalities can often be heard in departure lounges of airports or in hotel bars, exchanging fish-tale stories which reveal their prowess or preparedness to use their power to someone else's disadvantage.

It would be foolish to claim that this effect should be totally ignored as all of us are motivated by success – or we would not want to be involved in negotiation in the first place. However, the last moral that should be drawn from successes is that they can be readily achieved *just* through a charismatic personality – or by smiling a lot and charming the opponent.

CASE HISTORY

A workshop delegate returned from a holiday in Tunisia and described, for his fellow delegates, the wonderful deal he had achieved in the local market at the resort where he was staying. Haggling over a leather coat, he described how he had pressurized the market trader by arguing about the price – even walking away – (and being followed down the street with urgent pleas to return) and ultimately settling on a price which was approximately half the original asking price. Did he obtain a good deal? The workshop group decided that, as a consumer purchase, the deal appeared to be a good one – but against what measure? Was the coat of the same quality skin and make-up as might be purchased in England? If not, how much cheaper should it be?

Obviously a commercial buyer might have the advantage of being able to place a quantity order – thus earning himself a corresponding quantity discount – but a professional product evaluation would reveal the quality of the skin and lining, not to mention the quality of the make-up. For example, how many stitches per inch have been used in the garment?

All in all, the group decided that the coat might not have been the amazing bargain the customer had first thought – but he declared that he was still very pleased with it. Would he have obtained a better deal if he had had more inside knowledge?

Evaluation of a deal will be largely affected by the quality of the initial preparation stage.

HOW TO PREPARE

Some people find the self-discipline of planning very difficult – they are active people, preferring to get on and *do* things! Actually, the process of sitting with a blank piece of paper, and endeavouring to note down all that we know about the case which is coming up, can be a salutary experience. It can reveal just how little we really know and how many assumptions we have already made.

A recent seminar group 'brainstormed' the points that they wished to know about *before* a negotiation meeting was fixed. The results of their deliberations are shown at the end of this chapter.

ASSIGNMENT 1

Draw up your list of points here and then compare your list with theirs:

All these points could have a significant influence on your discussion, and *your* confidence will be greater if you can be reassured that there will not be any unpleasant surprises raised in the meeting for which you do not have an answer.

RESEARCH AND SOURCES OF INFORMATION

Where could you obtain all the necessary background information? We considered a variety of information needs in the last chapter and now we are going to examine some possible sources. Add your own sources which are peculiar to your own work environment or business sector.

RECENT AGREEMENTS

What recent agreements might be used to benchmark this proposal?

What do we know about our market leaders and recent deals they may have struck?

What is the current profile of their standing in the market (share price etc.)?

What intelligence has been released to brokers that could have a bearing on this deal?

....

....

....

....

PUBLICATIONS

How/where can I find out more about these agreements? What is known in the public domain? (E.g. press, research panels, people involved etc.)

National and trade press may have recorded news of major deals. Trade associations and buying or affiliation groups may be able to provide introductions to organizations in your own sector which are prepared to reveal recent salary agreements etc. Who else could I ask? Why not start inside your own organization?

If financial data is not part of your own particular strength, why not consult someone senior in your finance department who may have heard some whispers through the credit reference agencies (or the financial press) about any trading difficulties being faced by opponent organizations. In large, continuing relationship/commercial deals it is common practice in many organizations to send for a copy of the firm's annual accounts for analysis. Apart from the data which has to be published for shareholders, these may reveal information on how they see the market in which you are working.

In industrial relations circles, some trade union groups have found it very valuable to invite management representatives to their annual conferences as this helps to communicate the issues on which their members feel concern – and their strength of feeling! Such opportunities are very rarely a waste of time. They provide a very valuable forum for testing the water and taking soundings of grass roots opinion. In large organizations, where up and down communication may be contaminated or filtered, it may be surprising what can be gained in both formal and informal meetings.

In very close markets, where everyone knows everyone else, trade gossip can be both valuable and potentially ruinous! Trade representatives can provide a valuable source of information about your (and their) competitors – which may provide interesting pointers towards future deals.

....

....

....

....

KEY 'INFLUENCERS'

Who are the 'influencers' in this field? Who may be influencing your opponents (and general level of expectations in this field)? What are they saying about the position *you* are facing?

Other commentators who are worth following include stock market analysts and university researchers. These people may have an agenda of their own but their role is to provide independent advice and information about *your* markets or industry. For the price of a lunch – or a telephone call – you may pick up a very useful line of enquiry, especially where you are considering an entry into untried waters.

Finally, the negotiator should develop good communications links inside the community. Local chambers of trade, business links and other business clubs can provide very valuable introductions – and this is also true of central government departments such as the Department of Trade and Industry whose officials work closely with industry on trade fairs, export missions etc.

....

....

....

....

FUTURE PLANS

What plans do the parties have for the future (e.g. new models/products, job restructuring, new recruitment or training plans) which might affect the value of the product or service affected by the current deal?

Who might be prepared to divulge such information? Obviously not a top executive in the organization! However, there are very few *real* secrets in the world and there is usually someone around who will answer a subtle question – usually a junior employee who has not been asked/told to keep quiet about the new drug being tested, the plan to automate the largest production line, or the intention to open up a direct banking link with customers using home-banking technology (modems and lap-tops).

This is not foul-play – simply good research – but it should be remembered that, while you are researching your market – or your competitors – they are probably doing exactly the same to you.

....

....

....

....

SETTING GOALS OR OBJECTIVES

Negotiation has one major disadvantage – it can make people unhappy if they are unable to achieve what they think is a good deal.

Unrealistic goals are generally no more achievable in the hands of a highly skilled negotiator as realistic ones in the hands of untrained negotiators!

After all, we would think that there was something very wrong if we were offered a Mercedes at the price of a Mini (or a terraced house at the price of a mansion). So, the planning phase is important for negotiators who want to improve their results, have aspirations for above-average results and need to demonstrate their ability to develop a successful track record. Reality shows that all negotiators should give considerable attention to their:

■ 'shopping lists' (or goals);
■ the priority level of each item on the list;
■ parameters for each item – identifying the ideal and fall-back positions which they seek.

(The best representation of this method is through the building-blocks approach, illustrated in the next section.)

The following chart illustrates the interface between the research and preparation stages and the later negotiating sequence. It should be remembered that the data collected as part of the research phase will need to be redeveloped into usable notes for the meeting itself.

Full credibility is only achieved when the case is marshalled succinctly and is then presented astutely and assertively. Prepared notes should assist, not hinder, this process!

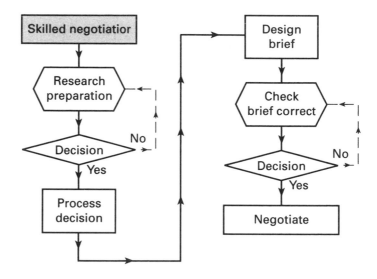

CASE EXAMPLE

The first task is to establish the negotiator's objectives for the meeting. For example, a retail buyer might be concerned to obtain:

❏ Price
❏ 'Elite' stockist status
❏ Quantity
❏ 'Top-up' orders
❏ Delivery
❏ Credits
❏ Payment terms
❏ Promotion allowance

The next steps are to set objectives against each category and to prioritize the checklist:

❏ a **cost price** which enables the product to be sold at an attractive selling price for the firm's customers – still earning the planned profit margin;
❏ 'calculated risk' status for a committed **quantity**;

> ❑ phased **delivery** – with monthly intervals – in March, April and May;
> ❑ 'top-up' **deliveries** to be available/honoured if the product sells well;
> ❑ **payment terms** of 45 days or longer;
> ❑ a **promotion allowance** to boost sales, through advertising, demonstrator, and/or free stock;
> ❑ 'no fuss' **returns policy** on any faulty items;
> ❑ **'elite' stockist status** awarded – opening up the opportunity for better terms in the future and help with factors such as fixturing, merchandising etc.

Additionally, the buyer might look back at the past season and check if all outstanding account queries have been dealt with – credits passed etc.

The buyer's brief

This listing may now be turned into a buying brief by charting the parameters of each objective identified on the 'shopping list'. Here, we need to establish the **most favourable position** (MFP) and **least favourable position** (LFP) for each item on the list, and the following chart illustrates how this might be completed:

Buying objectives	*Paramerters* Buyers' position — MFP ....LFP	*Selling objectives*
Price >	£5.50 (MFP) .... £6.25 (LFP) per piece	**Price**
Quantity >	500 pieces (MFP)................... 1000 pieces (LFP)	**Quantity**
Deliveries >	Phased delivery (4 months)...........two deliveries	**Deliveries**
Promotion >	£500 advertising allowance........display materials	**Promotion**
Terms >	60 days (MFP)...............................30 days (LFP)	**Terms**

| Returns | > | 'No fuss' credit ....selective credit by report | Returns |
| Status | > | Elite status awarded ....promised by next year | Status |

The seller's brief

It is probable that the seller is going through much the same process – reflecting the supplier's trading policy and aiming to develop the account. The following chart might be the result:

Buying objectives	Parameters Seller's position LFP .... MFP	Selling objectives
Price	£6.00 (LFP) ....£6.75 (MFP) per piece	Price <
Quantity	650 pieces (LFP).............. 1500 pieces (MFP)	Quantity <
Deliveries	Phased delivery .... one delivery	Deliveries <
Promotion	50/50 advertising (max. £100)........................ display materials	Promotion <
Terms	45 days (LFP)...........................10 days (MFP)	Terms <
Returns	...........Selective credit by independent report	Returns <
	Commitment to pay-up .... payment in 10 days	Account query <
	To sell across the range in larger quantities than last year	Range <

THE OVERALL PLAN

Of course, both sides need to plan for the possible objectives sought by the other side – and a good way to do this would be to merge the two sets of objectives on the one plan:

Buying objectives	Parameters	Selling objectives
Price >	£5.50 ....£6.25 £6.00 (LFP) .... £6.75 (MFP)	**Price** <
Quantity >	500 pieces (MFP).............. 1000 pieces (LFP) 650 pieces.................................. 1500 pieces	**Quantity** <
Deliveries >	Phased delivery (4 months) ....two deliveries Phased...one drop	**Deliveries** <
Promotion >	£500 advertising allowance ..display materials 50/50 advertising £100 max. ....Disp. mats	**Promotion** <
Terms >	60 days (MFP) ....30 days (LFP) 45 days.....................................10 days	**Terms** <
Returns >	'No fuss' credit ....selective credit by report selective credit by independent report	**Returns** <
Status >	Elite status awarded .....promised by next year	
	Commitment to pay up ....payment in 10 days	**Account query** <
	To sell across the range in larger quantities than last year	**Range** <

The great advantage of this approach is that it focuses attention on the areas of possible overlap in the positions of the two parties –

and therefore illustrates the negotiation opportunity. It is possible that the last three categories may only appear on one of the party's plans – and they may be unexpected by the opponent (suggesting that the negotiators will need to expose these agenda items during the meeting and 'think on their feet' when necessary).

A SERVICE EXAMPLE

An alternative example for this planning approach could demonstrate the issues involved in a service oriented contract. The client in this case might wish to negotiate a long term service contract for the maintenance of its building complex in a city centre. (The aim has been to reduce the organization's head count by sub-contracting rather than employing the appropriate tradesmen). The overall brief might result in the following plan:

Client's objectives		Parameters	Contractor's objectives
Charges	>	Hourly/Daily/Per Job Standard/Emergencies	**Charges** <
Reliability	>	of attendance Agreed plans diarized and committed	**Reliability** <
Staffing	>	Nominated staff only Agreed trades contracted in advance	**Staffing**
Quality	>		**Quality** <

Payment		Payment
>	60 days	
	14 days	<
Insurance		**Insurance**
>	All employees and work to be covered, as well as consequential damage Client to cover all related risks	<
Suppliers >	Nominated suppliers only Materials on client's account Complete freedom in buying	<
Sub-contractors >	Only approved firms allowed on site Complete freedom in emergencies	<
Standards >	Uniforms/politeness Timekeeping/clearing-up/ inspection to ISO9000 Normal management supervision applied	**Standards** <

ASSIGNMENT 2

Using the above approach, plan your objectives for a forthcoming meeting. Where you are unable to complete the objectives of your opponent there is an obvious need to research the 'gap':

Obectives	Parameters	Objectives

SETTING PRIORITIES

The final task in the preparation phase is to categorize the objectives in the listing. The purpose of this is to prioritize into:

- must achieve;
- should achieve;
- could achieve.

This should help negotiators defend themselves against being manipulated into accepting some conditioning on issues which are rated as (very) important on their list. (In the next chapter we will consider how to *use* this planning approach in the early stages of the meeting itself.)

CASE HISTORY

Another advantage of the use of this form of negotiating plan is that it also provides a valuable means of monitoring the progress of an agreement. Either negotiator could use the plan *after the meeting* to check that what had been planned – and then agreed – was actually implemented.

A company decided to sell its corporate training centre and, before making sealed bids for it, potential clients were invited to visit the complex. One tenderer was much attracted by the collection of engravings shown on the walls of the building and assumed that these were included; their bid was subsequently accepted but they were disappointed to discover that the pictures were not included in the sale. Their agreed bid had taken account of the estimated value of the pictures – and the discovery was only made when they came to take possession.

Skilled negotiators always do their homework *before* negotiating!

SEQUENCE PLANNING AND LINKAGE

Before the meeting, negotiators should think about tactics which might be used to help persuade the other parties to accept the objectives listed in the plan. One way of doing this is to consider how some items on the listing might be linked – an obvious example of this would include offering a higher quantity of stock items on the order in exchange for a lower price level.

Similarly, the desire for 'Elite' stockist status in the example above, may be exchangeable once a given level of business has been reached. Some of these exchanges may be predictable from earlier meetings – or perhaps from experiences of negotiations with other buyers or sellers – but ultimately the connections and their value, in terms of persuasiveness, will be decided by the way in which the discussion unfolds. Whilst this might appear to provide the best way of approaching the meeting, the fact is that skilled negotiators rarely plan to use their bargaining counters in a **fixed** pattern. After all, who wants to feel that they have been manipulated by a preconceived pattern which assumes that you will 'fall' into a pre-planned strait-jacket? Many people find the approach of selling-to-a-formula somewhat insulting to their intelligence – and develop a strong resistance to this approach. Fixed negotiation patterns can generate the same kind of feelings and are therefore usually left as the province of the less experienced negotiator.

WHAT IF IT ALL 'GOES WRONG'?

Obviously, the planner will be hoping that the meeting will produce a good result – but, in every field, there is always the possibility that no satisfactory agreement can be reached. For this reason the person should prepare at least one **alternative strategy** to follow; this will ensure that, given the absence of a fallback position, the negotiator is not pressurized unreasonably to accept an unattractive deal.

So, the best alternative to a negotiated agreement in the deal sought by the retail buyer in our earlier example could be provided by an alternative supplier – or another product range altogether – or perhaps the floor space should be re-allocated to a completely different department?

KEY TECHNIQUE: A PLANNING TREE

The group's 'brainstormed' plan at the start of this chapter produced factors which have been re-drafted into the following diagram which uses the 'mind-map' approach. It is claimed that this format makes the issues easier to remember.

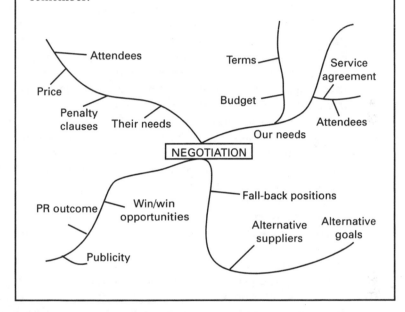

PROGRESS TOWARDS THE 'BETTER DEAL' – SUMMARY

After all the emphasis placed in this chapter on the value and importance of thorough research and sound preparation it might seem unnecessary to provide yet more reinforcement for this theme. However, one of the main distinguishing factors which divide *average negotiators* from those who achieve *outstanding results* – is the degree of preparation the latter group applies to their work. When the deals are relatively low-key or when there is little at stake and time is in short supply it may be that the depth described is considered something of an 'over-kill'. In such circumstances, maybe the deal should be delegated to a colleague whose time is less precious at the present time.

Skilled negotiators explore *all options* in their preparation so that they have already prepared for issues likely to be raised by the other party(ies). This knowledge should ensure that negotiators have full confidence in their brief – which should help the presentation and discussion of the case.

They also concentrate their planning effort on areas of potential common ground between the parties as these are likely to help in the search for concessions which will enable objectives to be met. The other perspective considered is that more attention is given to long-term issues, as well as the short-term ones, on the basis that the deal sought will be a win/win deal – contributing to the development of goodwill in the longer term.

All this concentration on the 'shopping list' approach to the preparation can cause the upper *and* lower limit parameters for each objective (as opposed to fixed points) to be overlooked. These are crucial points to determine as they identify the degree of flexibility in either side's position.

Finally, skilled negotiators are comfortable in discussing the agenda items in any order (rather than trying to push through a preconceived sequence). This flexibility enables the opponents to feel comfortable with the meeting – and not feeling 'strait-jacketed' into a fixed plan.

The best metaphor would be to match this approach with the skill of the juggler who is able to juggle eight balls in the air and determine which one to bring down at just the right time – without dropping any of the others. The mental agility required for this is fundamental to the opening and proposal stages in the meeting itself. Chapters 6 and 7 will help define these approaches for the reader.

6 *Opening and orchestrating the discussion*

INTRODUCTION

The research topics listed in the last chapter concentrated on the factors which related mainly to the *content* of the negotiation meeting. These will clearly be very important to the progress and outcome of the meeting.

However, meetings are often less effective because of the poor processes used – and this chapter will focus on some of the behavioural factors which can have a large impact on whether the meeting makes progress which satisfies both parties' needs and objectives.

Some of the difficulties in meetings are created by the 'comfort factors' involved in the meeting. These may involve:

■ uncertainty with the brief ('content' issues as described in chapter 5);

■ nervousness about the other person(s) (our and their expectations);

■ ability to cope with the other person's style and authority;

■ discomfort about the venue, seating plan, environment, atmosphere etc.;

■ insecurities about unexpected 'traps' and 'tactics'.

This chapter sets out some of the behaviours which are best avoided in our general pursuit of 'better deals' – and highlights those which should repay themselves in greater collaboration and win/win outcomes. We will consider how to make the best use of **opening tactics** through:

■ ice-breaking and

■ foreplay

and **orchestrating the discussion** through:

■ agenda planning and
■ speaking

especially in the early stages of the meeting.

OPENING

If the negotiation meeting is not to become one-sided, it is important that *both parties* should feel at ease. This does not mean that they should be casual or weak – simply that they should feel able to contribute to the meeting at the top end of their skills and with some anticipation that a good result can be achieved.

CASE HISTORY

At a recent workshop, 12 negotiators were asked where they preferred to negotiate – 'at home' or 'away'? Nine answered that they felt more in control 'at home' – of the remainder, two (sales representatives) preferred 'playing away' and the last person was undecided. If this was typical, everyone would probably seek to weigh their opponent's preferences – and endeavour to exploit their lack of comfort. As with likes and dislikes in other fields the best advice is to try to practise and find more advantages and likeable qualities in the things we least like – with the aim of becoming better at them.
Skilled negotiators are relaxed about playing at home or away!

When challenged, most people say that they feel more confident in familiar (home-base) surroundings where their security needs are met because they have ready access to notes/files/resources – and even a boss if additional 'weight' is needed. Actually, these points may just as easily work against the negotiator, especially if:

■ the office does not project the most organized or efficient image;
■ the 'home team' does not demonstrate a sense of mission;

■ it appears that negotiators can easily refer issues upwards for a 'final decision' – and may be expected to – raising doubts about their accountability levels.

Correspondingly, 'playing away' can give the visitor any number of opportunities for learning about the potential 'partner' and the business – simply by keeping eyes and ears open – and asking the right questions.

CASE HISTORY

A trainee retail buyer was visiting one of her firm's branded suppliers – as part of a planned learning programme – and she noticed that half of the factory floor was screened off. Naïve questioning revealed that the screens protected a special production line which was manufacturing for a major competitor (a variety chain store). At that time, the manufacturer thought that it would damage its branded business to announce this publicly and swore the trainee to secrecy. When he found out, the trainee's boss decided to stabilize orders with this supplier and spread more of the sourcing risks by increasing the number of suppliers in that sector. The information would probably have remained secret for a lot longer if the trainee had not made the visit.

Being the visitor provides negotiators with many opportunities to obtain additional data about 'opponents' – simply by careful observation!

Ice-breaking

Ice-breaking is just as important in a negotiation meeting as it is in any other kind of meeting. The opening pleasantries will help the parties to assess:

■ the mood of the other persons present;
■ their conversational and persuasion styles;
■ any indicators of who will be the person taking the ultimate decision (if more than one is present);
■ any explicit or implicit tensions which might affect the subject of the negotiation;

- topics or issues which may be of general interest and which may help form common ground for the people involved in the meeting;
- the extent to which the other person might be relaxed/influenced by a little flattery.

Mood

As we saw in chapter 4, the mood of your opponent may be very different from that which you might expect (perhaps from the initial contact that may have been projected from your telephone call setting up the meeting); perhaps, before your arrival your opponent has received a 'ticking-off' for something which has gone wrong (but not his fault) or, equally, the opponents are 'on a high' because of some very good trading news which has set an optimistic tone for the meeting. It is easy to be affected by these types of mood swings – and most would find it difficult to resist the thought that the happier the other parties seem to be, the more likely it will be for the two of you to reach agreement.

Painful mistakes have also been made by visitors to offices and, after assuming that the place of the meeting 'belongs' to the host, have tried to build common ground based on, say, a sailing picture on the wall. Subsequent conversation has revealed that the office actually 'belongs' to someone else! Such errors are easy to make – and embarrassing to recover from – even more so when the host has laid the trap deliberately! 'Ice-breaking' may be easily achieved with extrovert people – simply by the use of an 'open' question. For example:

Host: 'It's good to meet you at last. Did you manage to find us without difficulty?'
Visitor: 'Fine, thanks – the map helped a lot; it's a very impressive building, isn't it?'
Host: 'Well, I suppose so – except when the air-conditioning breaks down! It always seems to happen when you need it most, doesn't it?'
Visitor: 'Apart from that, are you keeping busy at the moment?'
Host: 'Stacked out! We're really stretched at the moment.'
Visitor: 'That's good – I assume it's our merchandise that's selling well!'
Host: 'I wish I could say it was! No, it's all the administration

Visitor:
Host:

> – you see, we are in the process of changing the computer and it's causing a few headaches!'

Visitor: 'How d'you mean – like loads of noughts on pay-slips?'

Host: 'No, nothing like that – but we have a few problems with the bought ledger which is slowing things down quite a bit!'

This revelation, at the beginning of the meeting, may just provide a useful defence when it comes to discussing the payment terms of a contract between supplier and client – especially if fast payment is used as a lever for better discounts.

Actually, the mood of a business meeting can make a big difference to attitudes to the business in hand – and marginal decisions – those 'shall-we-do-it-or-not?' situations which might go either way – are more likely to be handled optimistically when the players are feeling happy. (The Italians are renowned for this apparent spontaneity – which can be extremely enervating when one is used to the phlegmatic, careful approach more customary in northern Europe!)

It should always be remembered that critical or angry attitudes exposed at the start of a meeting may be used deliberately to stir up the visitor and incline them towards making concessions in the meeting. This approach might only be based on pretence, of course, as a tactic to 'soften-up' the visitor. In such cases, visitors should be careful not to lose momentum or their equilibrium but simply return good manners, patience and friendliness.

Conversation style

The dialogue above illustrates an important element of style. The host sounds friendly enough but he is also adept at prompting the visitor to respond by asking questions at the end of the early statements. This method is then mirrored by the visitor who 'wins' more information with the slightly flip remark about computer payroll problems.

Have you ever been to a party or social gathering and been buttonholed by a very pushy person? Maybe you found the person standing just a little too close (almost standing on your toes) and a little too talkative/extrovert? How did you react to this? Did you just want to escape?

Persuasion styles can vary from this extrovert example to a more inductive style using more questions and opportunities for the other person to speak. A more open communications style requires better listening skills – and provides for parties to a negotiation to learn about the other's needs. This does not mean that this style of debate will be *easier* – but certainly it will be less competitive. Contrastingly, two negotiators adopting a 'push style' might easily run into a competition for 'air-time' – and this can lead to conflict.

These indicators are important to identify early in the meeting as they provide a guide to the best style to adopt if interaction between the parties is to be successful.

Authority

In most sales training manuals, salespeople are urged to ensure that they make contact with the right 'MAN' – that is, the person with the M = money, A = authority to spend it, and N = need. The point is that it may be necessary for the other party to consult a more senior person if the bid is beyond his or her limit of authority.

Most of us try to conceal this fact since the alternative would be that all contacts would be made with the most senior executive in the organization and that person would be overworked with relatively small contracts and deals to negotiate (as well as the large ones).

Exactly the same principle applies to industrial relations negotiations where the somewhat unkind phrase 'it is generally better to negotiate with the organ grinder and not the monkey' is sometimes heard. The point is valid – it is best to keep at least some of your powder dry if you have to deal with a more senior executive in your quest for agreement.

Of course, from the other perspective, it is sometimes a useful strategy to erect a number of 'hurdles' for negotiators to jump over; more of their 'storyline' can be gathered by more junior managers – each of whom negotiate a partial deal by trimming the offer and then pass the issue up the line. The ultimate boss is then able to use all his or her authority to squeeze a much better deal. This tactic is readily spotted and less easy to avoid if considerable time has already been invested in the possibility of a deal (it may also be accompanied by promises of an even bigger deal, as the negotiator climbs the organizational ladder!).

These issues become even more interesting when the lone negotiator is confronted with two opponents; which one will have the final say – and what signals are they sending to you to indicate that the decision is turning in your favour or not, as the case may be? Subtle glances one to another or just a simple shift in eye contact may reveal increasing interest or just the reverse. Factors like this are important to notice in the early stages of a meeting as they may indicate pressure points for the later stages.

Foreplay

The early discussions at the meeting also constitute a form of foreplay between the parties. This activity may be affected by:

- seating and the environment;
- drinks to help relax the parties;
- sharing of 'news' of each party's organization;
- how the last agreement is being implemented (unless this is substantially the topic for discussion at the meeting);
- 'testing the water' for today's meeting by exploring the background to the current meeting;
- other 'safe' topics.

Seating and the environment

We have already seen that negotiating can be a subjective activity – we are influenced by our likes and dislikes for:

- our opponents and their organization;
- product presentation;
- colour and packaging;
- external factors (even including the weather);

so it should not come as any great surprise to learn that the decor, furnishing and seating can also create a considerable amount of influence on the participants.

Of all these factors, the most powerful can be a very simple matter of the seating position. The reader may have experienced differing levels of seating in a negotiation meeting and, the worry is, manipulation of this factor can work to one's disadvantage. (Or is it just a coincidence that the person on the lower chair is often the person who seems to end up making more of the concessions?)

Many businesses now provide 'neutral' meeting rooms which have been specifically furnished and prepared to neutralize the effects of colour, the clock, telephone and the layout. With complete flexibility over a seating plan, there is a lot to be said for avoiding a confrontational stance i.e. *not* face-to-face across a large desk.

A better layout would be to sit adjacent to each other – around a circular table, or perhaps across the corner of a desk. This might provide a slight problem for those who must have confidential papers in front of them as they negotiate – but even this can be accommodated if the figures are presented in code, for example.

So, what should negotiators do if they are uncomfortable in the room chosen for the meeting? First of all, if this is really serious (e.g. very hot, with no ventilation) it is always possible to seek an alternative room. If no alternative exists, perhaps the meeting can be reconvened on a different day and at a new location.

A seat which is too low – or which causes the visitor to face into the light – can be exchanged or replaced and, if there is a suspicion that this was a deliberate attempt to discomfit the visitor, an appropriate comment might also be made. For example:

Visitor: 'I notice my seat seems to be right in the sunshine. I'm afraid I will have to move it as I am allergic to ultra-violet rays!'

Food and drink

Hospitality can be a wonderful persuasion tool, but also exceptionally valuable in orchestrating short recesses in meetings. A drink at the start of a meeting provides a good atmosphere for welcoming guests/visitors. However, there are also some in-built dangers especially if papers and drawings have to be tabled and there are risks of accidents to them. Similarly, food can place the opponent at a distinct disadvantage if they attempt to eat whilst they receive a barrage of questions to answer!

Tensions and 'news'

The question of how to deal with sensitive issues, which might hinder the negotiations, also needs careful consideration. Careful tact and diplomacy are essential if painful nerves are not tweaked and uncomfortable reactions given. For example, after a serious fire at one of the company's sites it might be kind to sympathize about the difficulties that have been faced and gently enquire if the business is getting back to normal again. On 'bad days' a negotiator could find himself making some oblique reference to claiming the insurance money and how the company might now be able to build a 'proper, modern facility'! Such a remark might be intended as light-hearted banter or just a 'throw-away' line but it could be viewed by the other party as highly insensitive and create an immediate negative reaction. It would be easy for us all to claim that these are *not* traps we *normally* fall into – but we have all experienced moments when we have not been in total control of everything we say (this is sometimes described as 'mouth open but brain not in gear!').

It is not always possible to avoid sensitive issues which may have arisen in some private internal meeting – and the effect might be to witness the other party almost wince in pain. In such cases, there may be some background information to be gained from a naïve question hinting that the innocent person has not quite heard or understood something they have heard. This might bring some kind of explanation and it might be appropriate to offer an apology (for straying into an area of 'private grief').

Implementation

In continuing relationships, this element is one of considerable interest to both parties since there is bound to be a heavy focus on how previous agreements are being implemented. In the finance industries there has been a shift of attention to the concept and practice of compliance (meaning how we implement agreed policies and best practice) and, whilst few strictly commercial deals are subject to such rigorous scrutiny, a follow-up arrangement is bound to depend upon the success (or otherwise) of the implementation of previous deals. As we saw earlier, this should concentrate the minds of the parties *before* meeting – as part of their overall preparation. So, issues which might be raised may include satisfaction about:

- Quality of services or products supplied.
- Pricing structure – including accuracy of calculations etc. on invoices.
- Outstanding queries, credits, complaints etc.

■ How line representatives are relating with each other (in the two organizations).

Testing the water

At an early stage the parties may wish to 'test the water' of the subjects which will form the main topic for the forthcoming negotiation. This process is also sometimes known as 'fishing' for reactions to these issues. For example, if it is known that the opponent's boss has been away sick for some time and this has been quoted as a reason for the meeting to be delayed, some naïve questions about his or her recovery might be rewarded by some information about the response of the organization. For example:

Seller:	'I hear that your Operations Director has returned from sick leave now. Is he feeling better?'
Purchasing Manager:	'Yes, thank goodness, I don't know how we managed without him. But it did mean we had to pass more decisions down the line.'
Seller:	'So, does that mean that we have his blessing on the topic of today's meeting?'
PM:	'Well, as I am saying, we don't need it as we have reorganized some of his responsibilities and I report direct to the MD now.'

This revelation that the Seller is now dealing with someone just one step away from the 'seat of power' in the organization should be highly welcome and give an indication of increased accountability (and hopefully authority) ascribed to the Purchasing Manager.

'Safe' topics

As negotiators get to know each other better – and perhaps work together over a longer period – they will have more conversation subjects in common with each other. These bonds of experience are often of great value to both persons' organizations as either negotiator will know just what is possible to achieve as a result of, perhaps, years of working together.

There is, however, also the possibility of relationships becoming too close – resulting in negligible progress towards the real goals of either organization. Relationships *can* become too close!

CASE HISTORY

Russian and American negotiators had spent 18 months trying to negotiate peace talks at Geneva and no breakthroughs had been achieved. When the two great powers replaced their respective negotiating teams, a settlement followed very soon after.

Skilled negotiators avoid getting too close to the other party – they try to remain totally objective!

'Safe' topics for discussion during periods between formal negotiation sessions could include:

- the weather;
- recent holidays;
- sporting results;
- family activities.

This may seem a somewhat boring approach to interrelationships – but many a good relationship (in business and outside) has fallen down through the failure to apply this simple rule. It is also wise to keep off three other sensitive issues – politics, religion and ... sex!

Flattery

One way in which either party might encourage the other to think well of them is through the use of a small element of flattery. Many readers may be horrified by this remark and, of course, flattery can be both sincere and insincere! Insincerity is a poor way of impressing someone with whom one is trying to work – especially if it is readily obvious to them – and anyone else present. However, we all warm to praise and someone saying nice things is likely to create a slight softening in many people's resolve to stick to their negotiating brief. How important is this method to use and, if on the receiving end, how seriously should it be taken? Objectively speaking – not at all! (The present-day expression which makes this point is: 'He would say that, wouldn't he?')

ORCHESTRATING THE DISCUSSION

Setting the agenda

In many meetings, the agenda has been set long before the meeting has been convened; a trade union, for instance, will have made a written claim for consideration by the firm's management and this will form the central element of the agenda .

In commercial circles, the parties will have come together to discuss a new scheme, possibly, but it will help both parties if an agenda can be agreed to provide some shape to the meeting and ensure that goals can be met within obvious constraints (such as the use of time).

At the start of this book we also saw that a collaborative atmosphere (aiming at a win/win) is essential if the 'Better Deal' is to be achieved. This culture will not be achieved automatically – and it may be difficult if the opponent is a competitive negotiator at heart (who may be set on raising unexpected issues in the meeting – mainly to 'wrong-foot' you).

One way of avoiding this type of pressure is to agree the agenda at the start of the meeting. Indeed, in some negotiation meetings, a considerable amount of effort may be spent in trying to agree an agenda!

CASE HISTORY

Peace talks between the United Kingdom and the Argentine, following the Falklands war, were facilitated and hosted by the United Nations. However, it took many months of bargaining (behind the scenes) before agreement was reached about the agenda.

The main issue at stake was that Her Majesty's Government would not attend the meetings until they had cast-iron assurances that sovereignty over the islands was not on the agenda – nor would it be raised by the Argentinian delegation.

More recently, similar manoeuvring took place – and consumed considerable time – before the parties at the Northern Ireland 'peace forum' could agree their procedures and an agenda.

Skilled negotiators always try to influence the planning of the agenda – and prepare for it thoroughly.

Once agreement on the agenda has been reached, then 'new business' should not be introduced unilaterally into the meeting – unless this principle is accepted by both parties. (Apart from anything else, it will probably be on a topic which was *not* contained in the negotiators' preparations.)

Sequencing

The agreed, total agenda will now need placing into priority order and this is an important step before the negotiators move into the full discussion. There are no rules about which issues should seem to be predominant in the meeting except:

■ Issues which threaten to divide the parties should be dealt with earlier rather than later (so that areas of agreement should not be jeopardized by critical difficulties later in the discussion).
■ 'Harder topics' which require considerable concentration and care may also be better dealt with early when both parties are fresh and more likely to be listening and concentrating well.
■ Obviously some issues may link with others on the agenda and therefore this may indicate a preferred sequence. (However, it should be remembered that skilled negotiators avoid set sequences as these may indicate rigidity – the very opposite to the purpose of discussion and negotiation!)

SPEAKING – BEHAVIOURS AND ATTITUDES TO AVOID

Which brings us to the consideration of the behaviours which may create negative feelings in other people – in negotiation meetings, and outside! We will consider here:

■ Dogmatism
■ Brusqueness
■ Blocking
■ Irritators
■ Non-verbal communication.

Dogmatism

By this time the reader will appreciate that dogmatism will not bring a flexible response or easy agreement from the other party. This sounds easier than it may be in practice – after all, the preparation and rehearsal phase is all about identifying the better options to pursue in the meeting. The problem with this is that we tend to stick firmly to the one option which seems best to us and increasingly turn a blind eye towards those less favourable options. The net result is that we may become increasingly dogmatic about how much better our ideas are, rather than those of our opponents. So, what chance is there of agreement when two highly dogmatic people get together?

Brusqueness

Some people seem to think that to negotiate means to be abrasive, provocative and generally unpleasant! Their general line seems to be to court the possibility of a row – and, if confronted with malleable opponents, they may misuse their perceived power to intimidate and 'force' an agreement. The problem with this approach is that a short-term 'win' may turn out to be a 'lose' in the longer term when the person on the receiving end ignores the possibility of providing any useful advice or favours (which might save the person considerable trouble and expense).

There is a significant difference between being business-like and brusque. A business-like person avoids wasting time but recognizes the needs of their partner. These include:

- having their say in the meeting, and receiving a fair hearing;
- engaging positive eye contact and some warmth;
- feeling they are being treated as a human being!

Brusque people:

- are blunt and sharp, creating a negative reaction to them;
- appear 'off-hand' and this may be read as discourteous;
- are often 'propped-up' by non-assertive people who 'dig them out of holes'.

All this is dangerous in the longer game. When dealing with a brusque operator, the negotiator should:

- take deep breaths and avoid being roused;
- exercise lots of self-control, patience and self-discipline;
- retain the assertive communication style;
- concentrate on the issues and the options for agreement;
- call a recess if it appears that no progress is likely today;

■ avoid any expression of surprise if or when the opponent acknowledges some progress towards a deal.

Blocking

A 'blocker' is a person who responds negatively to suggestions but without giving any reasons – thus *blocking* any progress on the issue. For example:

MD: 'We would like to see your union ballot its members on these proposals which we feel are exceptionally generous.'

Convenor: 'We can't do that!'

MD: 'May I ask why not?'

Convenor: 'We don't do that.'

MD: 'Well, how are you going to know the views of the union members, then?'

Convenor: 'We have ways.'

MD: 'Yes, but do they work?'

Convenor: 'Yes, thank you!'

If this sounds like hard work – it is meant to! Blockers desire to place an obstacle in the path of any progress (unless of course it is something they want). The situation pictured above would have a more flexible feel to it if the convenor had given some reasons to explain his position. The MD may have had the impression that perhaps he did not know the answer but did not wish to reveal that.

CASE HISTORY

A senior executive in a leading plc made no secret of the fact that he would welcome the offer of early retirement. Having had this suggestion refused he became a human obstacle to many decisions in the business by simply blocking them. At meetings he would block many proposals and never give any reasons. Bargaining with him was impossible and the only common ground he had in discussion was Welsh rugby! Eventually he developed such a reputation for being obstructive that he was transferred into a job in which he could

> do little damage – and was then paid off! Ultimately, he got what he wanted; he won. For every example like this there are many others who have met a sticky end!
> **Skilled negotiators agree that reasoned disagreement is always preferable to blocking!**

Irritators

Irritators can be both verbal and non-verbal. We will consider the verbal ones at this point. Irritators are words or phrases which cause considerable irritation in the other person and, as irritation is not normally something which can be readily indicated without being aggressive or confrontational, it will probably mount up until it becomes obstinacy or just outright rejection. So, does this sound like an influencing skill to use? Definitely not! Buyers complain about sales representatives using expressions such as:

- unrepeatable/limited offer;
- special price;
- fair and reasonable;
- ultimate deadline;

and Sellers complain about Buyers' use of:

- the 'bar is up' (i.e. no more orders can be given);
- we do not have a budget for this/we are overspent;
- the Buying Director will not let me do it.

Longer-term promises can also generate irritation – such as the situation when the client uses a long-term offer to obtain a concession on today's business: 'Of course, if you can give me the price today, I will see that we look after you when the new contract is put out for tender.' This kind of promise is sometimes described as the 'golden carrot' – and, unless it is turned into something *much* more positive and formal, it is meaningless.

Non-verbal communication

The problem with 'reading' non-verbal behaviour is that it is a highly subjective topic. What may irritate one person may have little effect on another. However, here are some general rules to follow. Skilled negotiators avoid:

■ clicking retractable pens, or playing with calculators (or 'executive toys');

■ fidgeting around – drumming fingers on the table or wagging one foot or leg continuously;

■ staring out of the window – or at the ceiling – while the other party is speaking;

■ sniffing spasmodically;

■ speaking through their hands (indicator of non-assertiveness);

■ continually looking down their nose at the opponent (i.e. giving a feeling of being patronizing);

■ consistently frowning throughout the meeting (particularly off-putting – especially when coupled with the use of pessimism or 'blocking');

■ scratching themselves in embarrassing places (and other actions which may be read as 'bad manners');

whilst in a negotiation meeting.

TOWARDS THE BETTER DEAL

Skilled negotiators are very successful in using and controlling their speech and body language patterns to heighten their persuasiveness. This is not just the application of charisma or charm and switched on and off at will. It is a pattern of behaviour which creates warmth and support from the other party/ies and, generally, creates in them a wish to reach agreement in the meeting.

REVIEW ASSIGNMENT

The first five behaviours used by skilled negotiators were listed in chapter 3 – see if you can recall the definitions:

❏ Seeking information ....

❏ Testing understanding ....

❏ Summarizing ....

❏ Bringing-in ....

❏ Building and supporting ....

We are now adding three more, which are exceptionally powerful, and a reminder about the non-verbal signals to concentrate on:

■ **Behaviour labelling**. This means stating the behaviour you are about to use – before actually doing it. For example, 'I'd like to ask a question . . .' or 'Could I just clarify that point . . . ?'. The merit of this is that the other person is alerted to the behaviour which is about to come – and therefore concentrates and listens more carefully as a result.

■ **Revealing inner feelings** can also be an exceptionally powerful tactic – perhaps partly because it is so rarely done in meetings. For example: 'I really must say that I am feeling increasingly frustrated by this meeting.' The probable response to this will be: 'I'm sorry, I don't quite understand', which leaves the way clear for: 'Well, so far in this meeting you only seem to be interested in stating *your* point of view – may I have the chance to present my organization's viewpoint?'

■ **Charm**. There is nothing wrong with using a little old-fashioned charm in negotiation – and it is *not* dependent on charisma for its effectiveness! Charm can be defined as influencing others by giving pleasure to them – and a little of this in a meeting can be exceptionally valuable. Perhaps this concept is viewed by some as a little old fashioned but there is no doubt that a little charm can make all the difference in persuading the opposition – especially if it seems really genuine.

The **non-verbal signals** to concentrate on are:

■ Positive eye contact.
■ Smiles.
■ Open gestures:
   – typically meaning hands opened in support of statements made, with palms upwards; this is taken to mean – no secrets – trust me!
■ Positive attention and stance:
   – sitting up straight, leaning slightly forwards suggesting interest and enthusiasm for the subject of the meeting.

POSTSCRIPT

This chapter has introduced the behaviours which can make all the difference towards achieving better results in the early part of a negotiation meeting. To cement these skills, they must be practised

– preferably in a low-risk situation (such as a low-key meeting, or role play on a training workshop). It should always be remembered that, in trying to introduce change in these areas, the participant should move carefully and without attracting too much attention to what is happening. (There is a risk otherwise that the opponent may recognize what is going on and also try to change tactics and enhance his or her skills to the reader's disadvantage.)

In our next chapter we will continue to focus on the interactive skills we can use to progress the meeting – this time in the ways in which we prepare and present proposals!

7 *Proposals and persuasion skills in negotiation*

INTRODUCTION

This chapter explores the methods which are used by skilled negotiators to persuade opponents to move towards their planned objectives; they vary from the simple exchange of preplanned concessions, and building of formal proposals, to speak/listen ratios and the whole art of signalling.

Whilst the sequence and presentation of these ideas may all seem obvious to the reader – actually *carrying out* these functions, in the 'heat' of the meeting, is not so easy, and keeping a clear head can be even more difficult.

In chapter 4 we saw that 'inexperienced negotiators often have difficulty in progressing a meeting from the maze of discussion towards the "finishing line" of a deal. They find it difficult to piece together the issues and are uncertain on how to gain their objectives without giving too much away'. Actually, everyone probably experiences this from time to time!

MOVING FORWARD WITH PROPOSALS

The 'foreplay' and 'general discussion' described in the last chapter gives the opportunity for the parties to tease out the degree of flexibility which either side may have towards the issues which are on the table. This debate may take two forms:

- A short discussion about the overall issues, followed by an attempt to reach agreement on each agenda item – one by one (limited linkage of specific issues may occur).

■   A fuller, general exploration of all the main agenda items *before* any trade-offs are attempted, leading to a summary of the areas of proposed agreement.

Of the two methods, the second requires more skill since the negotiators will be trying to keep 'all the balls in the air' and bring them all together in the final agreement – leaving nothing out, nor giving too many concessions.

In the case of the first method, the art lies in ensuring that, even if the parties 'trade' one objective for another as they progress through the agenda, there is a perceived 'fair' balance as they approach the final issue. A problem may arise if this issue becomes a solitary win/lose item – with no chance of an 'exchange' without returning to earlier topics which have already been agreed.

A similar problem can occur if Party A stalls on an issue (on which he or she feels to be on weak ground), seeking to delay discussion of the item until later. 'Later' may turn out to be in the closing stages of the meeting – when Party B may not feel like jeopardizing all the areas of agreement achieved so far, by digging-in on this one sticking point which Party A deliberately delayed.

Skilled negotiators always seek to leave themselves with a balance of items they can exchange – even towards the close of the meeting.

Proposals are the only method of moving a negotiation meeting forward and their successful use is affected by:

■   Appropriate timing.
■   Careful phrasing.
■   Use of concessions.
■   Packaging.
■   Signalling.
■   Listening skills and recognition of this behaviour.
■   Assertive behaviour.
■   Persuasive pressure.

Appropriate timing

There is a right and wrong time for proposals to be initiated and it is important to develop sensitivity to the best timing – too soon and the opponent may feel 'crowded' or pressurized – too late and the opponent may feel swamped with the details clouded by the mists of discussion. So how can we tell that we have reached the right moment for proposals to begin?

General discussion about an issue will have covered all the key points – the product, service or scheme will have been described in some detail – and maybe the participants in the meeting will have raised (and answered) a few questions. It is time to make up minds and the requests or offers of concessions begin.

In some circles it is argued that the longer the parties debate the detail, the more likely it is for the 'client' (if there is one) to go 'off the boil' – change his mind – and decide not to go ahead! People should not feel rushed (but neither should agreements be reached by making too many concessions). The incentive to agree should be maintained and *making proposals* is one way of doing that. One or other of the parties may say:

(i)   'How do you feel about all that?' Or
(ii) 'Well, that's all the detail covered. Are you ready to move onto how we could make it work in your case?' Or even
(iii) 'Should we now discuss how we might bring the new scheme in?' Or perhaps
(iv) 'I'd now like to suggest some ways in which we could bring long-serving employees into line with the new conditions.'

Each of these *bridging behaviours* offers a way of linking the discussion and proposal phases and could be analysed in the following ways:

(i)   A neutral question seeking information about the *feelings* of the other party has the effect of drawing the other person out – do they feel comfortable about everything so far and are they ready to move on to the next step? This option is most useful when the negotiator is most uncertain about the reaction which may be forthcoming from the other person and, because it focuses on feelings, it may trigger useful insights into their intentions.
(ii) An unambiguous question which requests a clear statement of readiness – and provides the opportunity to discuss difficulties if or when the other party identifies outstanding points. This approach is useful if the opponent appears to be a down-to-earth pragmatist – the response of the opponent at this

point is most important. A 'Yes' is the aim – but the body language or tone of voice should be carefully analysed. Did 'Yes' really mean 'No'? Was there the slightest hesitation? (The extrovert salesperson sometimes uses this method and it can lead to the shock of an outright rejection by the opponent in the end.)

(iii) A suggestion, phrased in the form of a question, and using the 'soft-sell' method implying that the other parties could suggest another route if they are not ready to consider proposals. The sentence construction – using the 'should' form (rather than 'shall') adds the feeling that maybe we 'should get on with things for fear of the accusation of time wasting which we could be accused of if we don't progress to the proposals stage'. This method could be used when the negotiator is more than 66 per cent sure that the other party *will* want to move on.

(iv) A positive proposal designed to move the *process* of the meeting along to the next stage. This approach would best be used where the negotiator is 90 per cent sure that the opponent will not reject the suggestion.

Each of these behaviours could provide the necessary incentive to move the discussion to the next phase. If, however, the other parties state that they are not ready, what should be done?

Firstly, the initiator might apologize for appearing a little presumptuous – and then *seek information* from the opponent as to why they are not ready. For example: 'I'm sorry, I didn't mean to rush you. Is there any other information I can help you with?' This method should help clarify the present position and the negotiator can always re-use one of the 'bridges' again, later on.

Careful phrasing of proposals and concessions

As already mentioned, proposals can be concrete and positive: 'I'll tell you what, we will buy the quantity you have quoted, providing you give us that top discount rate and deliver by the weekend.' Or they can be 'trial proposals': 'Well, how would this be? Supposing we were able to improve the volume on the order, perhaps your organization would be prepared to increase the discount value?'

The longer and slightly more tentative phraseology gives the hint of the *trial proposal* and this is intended to give the other party room to debate the ideas contained in it – if they so wish! Alternatively, acceptance of the broad idea will allow a more formal, concrete construction to follow and this will help to move the meeting towards its natural conclusion.

Phrasing of proposals should always be conditional – using the formula – 'If . . . then' – in other words: 'If you will do this for me, I will do that for you.' Clearly, this is likely to be most successful when the ifs and thens seem to be in reasonable balance – the following example is not very likely to be accepted. 'If I lend you the car to drive to the station, will you give me £1000?' Of course, the offer could be enhanced with the addition of extra concessions – 'And I will let you use it for your continental holiday and throw in a tankful of petrol.'

This begins to sound like a better balance (depending on where the holiday location is and its duration).

Packaging

Sometimes, it may be clear that the other organization(s) involved *need* a particular response from the negotiator. This might include, for example, an apology for a previous error or loss – and there is no way that the current debate will be resolved without a satisfactory outcome to the earlier issue. So, the final agreement may need an additional clause offering: 'Supplier X acknowledges the recent inconvenience experienced by the client which was caused by the irregular merchandise supply position and will discuss opportunities for joint promotions in the next season to compensate for possible loss of business opportunities.'

In reality, little has been offered here but the inclusion of the clause may go a long way to appease the client's boss who may be pretty sore about previous experiences.

Skilled negotiators remember that they are always negotiating at two levels – the first is with the other representative, the other is with that representative's organization!

This sometimes explains why one objective is unlikely to be conceded by the other side – it breaches the inhibitions or fundamental policy of that organization (at this time!). However, the goal may be achievable at another time – or place – or after a forth-coming reorganization etc.

Signalling

A signal is a phrase or expression which indicates a preparedness to negotiate over some aspect of the meeting's objectives. For example, the negotiator may say:

Buyer: 'We need a better price than you have offered so far.'

Seller: 'We wouldn't *normally* be able to improve the cost price, but . . . maybe there's something else we could do.'

The important word here is *normally*; it indicates the opportunity to the opponent that the current circumstances are not normal and therefore deserve a better offer. This could be the point at which the negotiator uses the 'power card':

Buyer: 'Don't forget that you're dealing with the firm that holds access to just about 35 per cent of the retail market – so we can help your firm make this range a real winner – especially if we can reach a deal quickly!'

If we are tuned-in to signals then we should be able to respond to the other party's needs. However, failing to respond to a signal can extend a meeting considerably.

Think about it. If you wanted to hint to your opponents that your side might be able to accept, say, a lower price – provided they improve their offer in some way – and they completely ignored the signal, how would you feel. Rejected? Confused? Concerned that you might be facing a trap? The result is likely to be a slow-down in the conversation until understanding or trust has been re-established. So, this could also be the effect on them if *you* lost concentration – and missed *their* signals!

Remember, too, that your opponent may be inexperienced or untrained, in which case there is a possibility that he or she will not recognize *your* signals. But how can you find out why? Here is yet another reason for finding out as much as possible about your opponent *before* the meeting.

Listening skills

The typical concentration span of the average person is about 45 minutes – but most of us would also agree that we lose attention quite a number of times during that period! This is quite a frightening prospect when the previous section on signalling is considered. Never mind whether we can recognize signals when they are sent – will our concentration be good enough actually to hear them? This section describes poor listening habits and then offers some ways in which listening skills may be improved. Here is a set of **poor listening habits** which may affect all of us at times:

■ **Making hasty judgements**

Do you condemn a subject as uninteresting without a fair hearing?

Do you 'tune-out' because you believe the speaker will have nothing interesting to say, or is long-winded and cannot contribute anything of value?

Do you 'jump the gun' on what the speaker is saying to you, or show impatience? Do you allow the negotiator to finish in his or her own time?

■ **Interruptions**

If you can guess the end of the sentence or remark, do you interrupt?

If you do, do you get it right or wrong? If you are puzzled or annoyed do you interrupt to get the matter straightened out?

Do you allow third parties to interrupt the conversation?

■ **Attention**

Do you let your mind wander or day-dream?

Do you try to make the speaker think you are paying attention when you're not?

Do you display signs of impatience or irritation, perhaps unwittingly?

Are you easily distracted by other sights and sounds?

If you can think four times faster than a person can talk, how do you use this excess time?

■ **Selective listening**

Do you turn a deaf ear to certain topics or subjects?

Do you only listen to certain people?

Do you only want to hear about the good things and not the bad things?

Do you refuse to discuss certain items because they are unfamiliar, or do you *think* they will be too difficult to understand?

Do you primarily listen for facts, rather than ideas, when someone is speaking?

Do certain words or phrases, or someone's appearance, prejudice you so that you cannot listen objectively?

Do you let someone's delivery or quality of speaking put you off?

So, how can we become better listeners? One way is to avoid the poor listening habits above! Another is to take some *positive action*:

KEY TECHNIQUES

Here are eight **positive actions** to take to become a better listener:

1. Try to find the presenter's subject useful, even if it does not attract you. Listen, and sort the wheat from the chaff.
2. Concentrate on the ideas, not the delivery or the side issues. It is the ideas that are important. Take notes if you need to.
3. Withhold your judgement until you have heard all the speaker has to say.
4. Be attentive, and put your energy into listening. Resist distractions!
5. While the other person is speaking, watch his or her lips; when speaking, watch their eyes!
6. Do not be afraid to tackle difficult topics or concepts. Do not avoid the uncomfortable or thought-provoking – accept the challenge.
7. Do not 'tune-out' because of words or ideas that are emotive to you. Do not let these stand between you and the message. Keep your mind open!
8. Profit from the difference between the speed of speech and the speed of thought. Use the spare thinking time to effect by anticipating, mentally summarizing, weighing up the evidence.

The thinking and evaluating process which the negotiator carries out whilst listening to the presentations made by the other party is illustrated in the following diagram.

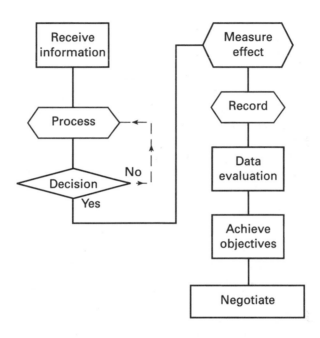

Not all the things you listen to are going to be interesting or worthwhile; there will be people who will waste your time; there will be impractical suggestions; there will be those who will bore you with pointless reminiscences; there will also be the exaggerator, the opportunist, the gossip, the politician, the inveterate complainer, and many more.

Listening can be trying! Remember that listening is something we need to encourage and foster in all those around us – as well as to set the good example!

Finally, it is worth remembering that persuasive negotiation does *not* mean that you have to do all the talking! The *inductive*

style of persuasion can be most successful with a 40/60 talk/listen ratio.

STAYING ASSERTIVE

Assertiveness lies between aggression on the one side and non-assertion, or passive behaviour on the other. Skilled negotiators try to be assertive throughout negotiation meetings because:

■ Passive behaviour attracts aggressive behaviour from opponents – they may be tempted to misuse their power (of personality, not just bargaining position).

■ Aggressive behaviour creates resistance – even when the other party has given tacit agreement in the meeting. (They may look for ways of unravelling the agreement *afterwards* and, if feeling particularly bruised they may look for ways of obtaining their own back next time! And so begins a tit-for-tat 'war' game!)

Being assertive does not mean being unpleasant; the communication style requires a combination of:

■ a firm, confident tone of voice in the meeting;
■ precise phraseology – saying what you mean, without waffle;
■ elimination of hesitancies – errs, umms etc.;
■ positive body language to support a business-like image.

So how can we maintain this style in negotiation meetings? The first keypoint is to recognize its importance in delivery and impact on the opponent and *want* to maintain this continuity by:

■ reinforcing confidence by ensuring thorough preparation before the meeting;
■ resisting intimidatory tactics (e.g. seating plans as described earlier);
■ avoiding the impact of status symbols – large desks, executive toys etc.;
■ using tactics, such as recesses, to 'regroup' if feeling under pressure and fearing that you might make concessions too readily;
■ concentrating on the validity of your case – bearing in mind that the research you put into it is credible and needs to be coherently presented;
■ trying to maintain an agreeable humour throughout the meeting.

PERSUASIVE PRESSURE

In addition to the use of the assertive style, negotiators may use additional persuasive pressure to encourage the other party to move closer to their position. These methods, whilst mostly readily identifiable, *can* dilute the negotiator's confidence and gradually reduce his or her resistance:

- **Conversational 'closers'** – for example the use of 'isn't it?', 'doesn't it?' at the end of selective statements which are designed to elicit agreement from the other person – 'You can see that we have come up with a really good proposal which fits the needs of businesses of your size – it's an attractive offer, isn't it?'
- **Coercive behaviour** emphasizes the potential power of the negotiator – for example, a large man might deliberately remove his jacket and slowly roll up his sleeves whilst speaking in a slow, deliberate and quiet voice – a woman might speak in an aggressive manner (in both tone and volume) – perhaps more associated with a masculine style.
- A **reward strategy** plays up the benefits which the opponent should experience as a result of reaching agreement on the proposals on the table. Overplayed it can be rather too obvious – and possibly obsequious!
- **Expertise** is something we all try to acquire and use in meetings – especially when we believe in our own preparation and case. However, there is always someone who knows more about it than us! We hope never to meet that individual in a negotiation but it *could* happen. So, making oneself thoroughly familiar with the case is the first requirement (but may still not be sufficient on its own if you know you are going to meet an acknowledged expert in the field).
- **Custom and practice** is often used as a strategy – to try to affirm a pre-prepared deal on the basis of 'We have always done it this way so we would find it very difficult to change now.' The 'old ways' may have gained legitimacy through approval by all those concerned – but it doesn't mean they cannot be improved! Of course, new ways *are* needed from time to time – there are always better ways of doing things – but they may not be 'better' if they disadvantage *you*!
- **Referent influence** is something we all practice in one way or another by trying to present ourselves to our opponents in the most

likeable of ways. Salespeople try to develop this approach by being optimistic, lighthearted characters – good fun to be with. This does not make the deal but it goes a long way and *can* work in both directions. Referent influence can also work in negative ways – for example, dress codes suggest that we should not ignore the inhibitions of the other parties. In the UK we may be excused for dressing up for a meeting with a managing director but rarely will we be excused for dressing down! In other words, don't choose to wear a pink shirt (men!) or trousers (ladies!) if you know the people you are to meet don't like them!

■ **Identification**. The reverse end of referent behaviour is where the other person models his or her appearance, behaviour and even speech patterns on yours. Initially this may not be noticed – and may simply achieve the desired objective – it might help you to feel more comfortable in their presence. The effect is similar to the process of identifying club members by their tie, scarf or badge and only becomes a concern when it goes unnoticed and may therefore be said to be working. It might be actually worrying if everyone else can surmise what is going on – but not the person on the receiving end!

■ **Compliance**. Most UK organizations have rules about gifts and corporate entertainment and these have been devised to protect decision-makers from objective decisions being clouded by issues of personal gain. Should individuals become tempted to break such a rule they may suddenly find themselves obliged to make decisions in favour of the 'influencers' in case the indiscretion is discovered. This may sound far fetched to some readers, but many others will be able to write their own case studies on this subject.

Skilled negotiators use their influence with others but do *not* generally employ dishonest tactics!

■ **Internalization** occurs when the other party uses ideas (and even words) which have been implanted in their minds a few minutes, hours or days ago. Your immediate response would be to react by drawing attention to the origin of the idea or thought. However, this may bring the influencing style out into the open and make it less easy for you to use it again in the future. (There is a down side to this strategy – if you are enjoying a period of high creativity you should ask yourself where those ideas have been coming from! It may be that *you* are internalizing *someone else's* ideas!)

RECONSIDER AND EVALUATE THE DEAL THROUGH A RECESS

With all these persuasion methods in use, proposals flying around and signals being sent it might not go amiss to recommend that progress towards the deal should be re-evaluated. If we were feeling quite sure about progress – and are happy with it – this may simply confirm our satisfaction. However, if the negotiator feels that there may be a 'hidden agenda' which has gone unnoticed, then a re-evaluation may be valuable. This could be achieved in two ways:

- the physical recess;
- the conversational recess.

Physical recesses

Calling a physical recess helps negotiators:

- collect their thoughts;
- consider ways of making more progress by using different tactics;
- regroup following a period of intense pressure;
- re-evaluate progress in the deal and any loose ends which might still be outstanding.

It should be remembered that this kind of recess does not necessarily bring any competitive advantage – since the opponent(s) will have had the same opportunities for regrouping etc.

Conversational recesses

The conversational recess occurs when one of the parties changes the subject – during the debate – to a topic which is of common interest to the other party thus distracting them from the current state of play in the meeting. Some people might find this distracting (as described) or even confusing (its probable intention). If the reader should be on the receiving end of this tactic, the best response is:

(a) to note down an *aide memoire* for the current position in the discussion;

(b) to take part in the new topic as if it is the most natural thing to do;

(c) to return to the original discussion – making doubly sure that the opponent does not mistake the re-entry point (accidentally or deliberately).

This manipulative approach to influence can add to the charm of the opponent – it can become an interesting diversion to the main meeting. However, it can also be potentially dangerous!

BEHAVIOUR AND SKILLED NEGOTIATORS

Overall aims

Skilled negotiators follow a pattern of behaviours and qualities which contribute to:

- clarity;
- persuasiveness;
- deals which can be readily and successfully implemented;
- the long term and a successful track record.

Behaviour avoided

They also try to avoid the following *competitive* behaviours:

- Counter-proposals – offering the direct opposite to the previously offered proposal (black versus white, right versus left, morning versus night etc.).
- Disagreeing – reasoned statements of why a position or proposal is unacceptable can have a negative influence on the meeting, making it less likely that an agreement will be reached.
- Defence/attack spirals – which create competitive debate and can lead to tit-for-tat behaviour.
- Argument dilution – where negotiators dilute the power of a proposal by linking several supporting arguments (both strong and weak) – each of which progressively weakens their case, through inviting the other party to attack the weaker arguments.

TOWARDS THE BETTER DEAL – REVIEW

Skilled negotiators try to use the following characteristics in their bargaining:

- Enthusiasm – encouraging the other party to see all the benefits of the deal.
- Determination and high aspirations.

■ Ability to resurrect stalled or rejected issues.
■ Supporting ideas and proposals offered by their opponents (even when they wish to disagree with them) – in other words they make disagreement sound like agreement!
■ Building on others' ideas – to help turn them to their advantage.

REVIEW ASSIGNMENT

An important assignment at this stage is to observe a *real* negotiation – perhaps with a colleague or a more senior executive – tracking the number of the following behaviours used in the meeting by your colleague:

Behaviour	Colleague	Opponent
Proposals		
Concessions		
Hesitancies (umms/errs)		
Conversational 'closers'		
Conversational recesses		
Supporting		
Building		
Resurrecting issues		

Our consideration of the negotiation structure pauses in chapter 7, while we examine the complications which can be experienced when negotiations are 'played out' in teams – especially between unprepared or untrained 'players'.

8 Negotiating in teams

INTRODUCTION

So far we have examined negotiation mainly from the perspective of individuals – 'one-to-one' negotiation. The processes involved may have seemed potentially complicated, or even hazardous, but the reader should find the skills capable of being developed through the various set assignments. When two people meet together to negotiate, we have seen that the outcome will be affected by a wide range of factors – not least the frame of mind and degree of competitiveness which either party may bring to the meeting.

Once *additional people* attend the meeting, a completely new dimension comes into play since all individuals may have their own agenda and certainly their own views on the methods which might be employed in the meetings. There is also the fact that the dynamics of a meeting tend to change in geometric proportions according to the number of people attending.

This chapter, then, offers an insight into the challenge of team negotiation and sets some standards for behaviour of participants. Having said this, the interactive processes involved in meetings can create power for constructive, and destructive, results. If a positive result is to be achieved, it has to be said that good control of the *processes* used at the meeting, is essential. We will consider:

- Team leadership and roles.
- Mission and belief in the case.
- Orchestrated use of specialist inputs.
- Strategies for recesses – fluency and concentration.
- ' Multi-speak' and team behaviour.
- Presentation skills.
- Communication inside the team.

TEAM LEADERSHIP AND ROLES

Each team in negotiation meetings *must* be led by an accountable person. If this is *not* done there is a risk that the interaction processes overtake both the objectives and plans of either party. It will be much more effective if the meetings are under the full control of the leaders – especially when the other people at the meeting become uninhibited and over-enthusiastic (even provocative). The leader may not necessarily be the most senior person present in that team; provided he or she has a clear brief (and thorough understanding of their authority) – in fact, sometimes, the devolution of divisional or departmental responsibility may be a useful tactic should some fallback position be needed later if deadlock is reached (further meetings can then be held at a 'higher level', which may enable new tactics to be employed – or concessions found – without compromising the integrity of either team). So, what role should the leader contribute?

Many books have been written about leadership, and the qualities of effective leaders provide a good starting-point for team negotiators – being able to contribute some or all of the following 'top ten' qualities to the team leadership role will help bring successful results:

ASSIGNMENT

Key insight: 'top ten' qualities of effective leaders
See how you feel your skills and qualities match up to this important set – compiled by a group of top managers from commerce and industry:

❑   Ability to take decisions
❑   Integrity
❑   Enthusiasm
❑   Imagination/vision
❑   Willingness to work hard
❑   Analytical ability
❑   Ability to spot opportunities
❑   Understanding of others/empathy
❑   Ability to meet unpleasant situations

> ❏ Ability to adapt quickly to change.
>
> How do you match up? Could you cope with pressure on all these during a particularly long and arduous series of team negotiations? If you have some doubts then you ought to devise a self-development programme in conjunction with your immediate manager/director.

John Adair's action centred leadership model (from his book *Action Centred Leadership*) concentrates on 'Task, Team and Individual' – providing a useful framework for mental preparation for the leader. It may also give some useful insights into potential challenges which may arise during protracted team negotiations.

Whichever preparation framework is adopted, probably the most important skill an effective leader can bring to this task is being able to inspire the team (and hopefully the opposing team as well!). This will be helped considerably by the ability to produce and 'sell' his organization's vision of the future.

Leaders may choose to take the major presentation role and lead the team 'from the front' – relying on the rest of the team to undertake supporting roles. Alternatively, the leader may fulfil the role of chairperson, co-ordinating the various inputs to be provided by the team. The second approach is the more challenging of the methods – since greater preparation and instinctive understanding is required between team members. This may be gained largely by working together over a period of time and, with less experienced teams, should involve systematic and thorough rehearsal. Roles of the team might be distributed to include:

- the immediate deputy (valuable in cases of protracted negotiations or where the leader may be called away);
- the 'secretary' – preferably someone who has the facility to record all interactions (which is especially valuable where the phraseology of offers and proposals needs to be carefully logged);
- the observer (briefed to look for and analyse non-verbal behaviour);
- 'experts' with specialized inputs.

Many a court case has come to grief where an 'expert' has been called to give evidence in support of a case – only to have his whole credibility destroyed by the opposition. A negotiation meeting may not always be quite as exacting as a court of law but it is still possible for a specialist to destroy his own side's case, if not under the proper control of the team leader – by getting excited, over-stating his case, and revealing factors best not mentioned – or perhaps by diluting his own argument with too much detail.

Observers' input needs to be taken into account during recesses – especially if they believe they have picked up 'evidence' which may indicate opponents' discomfort with the brief, statements made, sensitivity with some of the issues raised, or dissembling.

The contribution of the secretary is to help identify incon-sistencies in the opposing team's strategy or beliefs, and to track the offers and proposals made. This latter detail is important – espe-cially when it comes to the close of the meeting and the exchange of documents. It is at this point that the legal issues may need to be clarified, and the details checked. Unfortunately, many apparently excellent deals have turned into disasters when the 'small print' has not been checked and agreed.

Many negotiators find themselves moving towards the role of one-man band; given the organization's need for continuity, this is clearly quite unacceptable. The best deals are generally constructed after considerable team effort and debate, and the support of a deputy is very valuable when energy levels are diminished.

MISSION AND SELF-BELIEF

It is often said that the most difficult people to negotiate with are hijackers! This is because they have a deep conviction about their cause – and probably little concern for their own safety (or even survival).

So, an important starting-point for all teams of negotiators is the development of complete loyalty and support for the case being negotiated. The less certain the team may be about their case, the more likely that they will find themselves identifying with their opponent's case and giving away (as opposed to trading) conces-sions. So, how can 'belief' be created?

■ Firstly, the strengths (and potential weaknesses of the case) should be carefully prepared, and the strong points deliberately reinforced – especially for team members!

■ Secondly, the best ways to present the strengths should be considered so that the reverse side of each issue is not immediately invited as a response from opponents through the chosen presentation method.

■ Lastly, through role-play, the strengths of the case should be reinforced, through repetition, to heighten the commitment of each team member (role play also provides opportunities for role reversal which may enable the exposure of cracks in the case of either party involved).

This approach brings with it the obvious opportunity to invite colleagues to rehearse the negotiation meeting itself, so that the probable arguments to be used by the opponents may be identified. This will then enable the search for counter-arguments, and ways of weakening each issue to be found.

During the meeting itself, the team observer should be looking for non-verbal signals of commitment and self-belief (or, perhaps more valuable, lack of it!) in opponents. These signs might include an individual:

■ adopting a 'laid-back' position after previously using an enthusiastic, leaning forward pose – perhaps also shifting seating position so that his or her body is angled away from the focal point of the meeting;

■ doodling;

■ showing a sceptical facial expression – perhaps even showing disapproval.

These will be helpful signs of disenchantment in the team and create opportunities for grasping the initiative in the meeting.

CASE HISTORY: APOLLO 13

When it seemed most unlikely that NASA ground control could engineer the safe return of astronauts Jim Lovell, Fred Haise and Jack Swigert, the support team appeared to have completely lost heart – and be contemplating the consequences of failure. Flight Director Gene Kranz then imposed

> his authority by setting new goals for each functional team with clear objectives and timescale for the preparation of a crisis plan to secure the crew's return. The public exchanges and negotiations between each functional team and the Flight Director helped to re-impose some discipline and sense of purpose in the midst of a crisis. The resultant think-tank activity brought workable plans which ensured the ultimate safe return of the crew – on what would otherwise have been a doomed mission.
> **Skilled negotiators' sense of mission is quickly transmitted to the rest of the team – especially with critical, life-and-death decisions!**

ORCHESTRATED USE OF SPECIALIST INPUTS

Individuals in the team will probably have specialized 'portfolios' reflecting their job/function responsibilities. For example, a company team seeking to negotiate a reduction of their labour bill by introducing new technology could include:

- Chief executive – acting as leader.
- Operations director – dealing with the adoption of new technology/machinery.
- Personnel director – covering the skills/manpower needs.
- Works manager – providing detailed support on shift patterns (if required).

A trade union team might mirror the management team with:

- Regional (or national) organizer – acting as leader (with experience of negotiating such issues at other sites).
- Chairman of local union branch – providing historical perspective of issues at this site.
- Chief staff negotiator – major spokesperson for the branch with detailed understanding of the members' needs, aspirations and depth of feeling.
- Secretary of union branch – capable of providing records and observations of the meeting.

In addition, either team could wish to call upon the services of 'experts' who can provide specialist inputs on the use of the new equipment including:

■ Possible health and safety issues involved.
■ Requirements for retraining of existing workforce (and the likely costs).
■ Disadvantages/advantages of contracting-out services such as equipment servicing.

Clearly, such expertise can be readily 'neutralized' in argument by 'experts' marshalled to present the opposite case in the meeting (a method which is readily identified in public planning enquiries). Over and above these 'expert' roles in the meeting, team tactics may include operation of specific roles such as 'good guy, bad guy' routines. These can be effective as persuasion methods, provided:

■ the players make them credible;
■ the tactic is shown to be under the control of the leader.

This formal approach may not contribute much to creative thinking processes which can be so valuable in team preparation and recesses. Free-ranging discussion (and techniques such as 'brain-storming') may produce more creative ways of handling difficulties – especially from participants who may not 'own' the problems themselves.

CASE HISTORY

Security organizations who have been delegated the task of negotiating with bank robbers and terrorists for the release of hostages, often use the support and advice of psychologists in their bids to bring crises to a peaceful end.

A key technique is to reduce the opponents' vision and expectations by painting a picture of the poor chances of any more positive outcome than surrender. This action, directed against the security needs of the opponents, has been known to be successful against all but the most fanatical of terrorists. **Skilled negotiators are accustomed to attempting to reduce the expectations of opposing teams.**

STRATEGIES FOR RECESSES – FLUENCY AND CONCENTRATION

As we have seen, the recess provides a useful opportunity if the team needs regrouping before making a response to proposals (which need a little more than instant thought and reaction). In team meetings, both needs can make a physical recess an absolute imperative.

In cases of obvious disagreement inside the team (for example, with one member clearly wanting to accept proposals whilst another may wish to refuse them) or where there is a need to talk through the effects of a new offer on the team's strategy – away from the gaze of the opponents, a recess will be the best way of consulting and re-forming group strategy.

This demonstrates one vital factor – will the recess take place in a 'clean' place (i.e. without the risk of either observation or being overheard)? If not, the team may need to consider how to distract the attention of the opponents – perhaps by one member socializing with the opposing team while the rest go into discreet consultation. (By the same token, the hosts may have an in-built advantage if the recess deliberations just happen to be overheard!) So, there are several situations in which a recess may be valuable:

■ If a new proposal from the other team requires consideration before receiving a serious response – especially if it raises issues which the team has not previously considered.

■ When a message arrives which the team wishes to consider – and, especially, how it might impact on the negotiation.

■ To gain the initiative by delivering some new message designed to provoke a change in behaviour or response, followed immediately by a request for a recess (this tactic is valuable when the opponents have been blocking progress or are being stubborn).

■ To provide an opportunity to restore concentration when one or more of the team members is finding it difficult to maintain fluency.

A useful tactic to remember when using recesses is to precede the break with a summary of the current position. This should help concentrate the minds of both teams on the issues which still need attention.

When the teams reassemble, a summary will provide clarity and a useful 'join' between the earlier sessions and the current one; a statement of a new agenda should then be agreed to redirect the discussion in the new session.

Recesses should not be too long; the danger is that the break seriously reduces the momentum of the meeting and it would not be unknown for one team to be furiously debating the next moves, whilst the other is planning what to have for lunch – or the agenda for the next board or union meeting!

CASE HISTORY

The pressure of time can be a most compelling negotiating lever which can create movement when none previously seemed possible. This approach has been known to fail, however, when it takes the form of an ultimatum (for example, 'Withdraw your forces from Ruritania by midnight on 31st October to avoid a declaration of war' – use of the 'compliance strategy') it may be more successful.

However, where a team of creditors is pressurizing a company for its money and bankruptcy can only be averted by a refinancing deal (providing new sources of working capital), boards of directors have been known to sign away valuable equity in the company to provide a survival solution. In such circumstances, realistic timetables need to be agreed to allow sufficient time for a win/win solution to be found – without the risk of the crisis or loss becoming worse.

When survival is at stake, and options are scarce, skilled negotiators need time for recesses to consider their *best* options – and maybe investigate alternative strategies.

MULTI-SPEAK AND TEAM BEHAVIOUR

How formal should interaction be in the meeting? Speeches *at* opponents might satisfy egos but they do not win friends and influence people! Here there is a dilemma – without some formality, control may be sacrificed; too much formality and interaction may be stilted and lacking in real flexibility. So, it is important for some interaction rules to be followed.

Experience shows that, unless there is a formal plan to the contrary, the exchange of conversation by the team leaders tends to be followed by the entry of one of the 'seconds' who, in due course, is followed by his or her opponent. The danger of this 'social approach' is that individuals down the line may join in the discussion (and even set side-shows going of their own!) with no particular strategic aim or relevance to the meeting's objectives.

Without control, there is a danger that the meeting descends into chaos; the simplest form of this is multi-speak – a term which describes more than one person talking at a time – thus making it impossible for the interactions to be heard (let alone understood and responded to). This effect is particularly noticeable with excitable people or nationalities.

CASE HISTORY

A group of client executives working for a leading marketing agency in Greece were undertaking a team negotiation exercise on a training workshop involving two teams of three negotiators. Within five minutes of the start of the task, all members were speaking at the same time – making it quite impossible for any listening to occur! Everyone agreed that this type of behaviour was ineffective and committed themselves to take a more controlled approach next time! The next exercise required a similar approach (three against three) and identical behaviour occurred!

Some cultures have created in-grained patterns of interactive behaviour which can be very difficult to change; skilled negotiators recognize this and compensate with greater self-control and patience when dealing in foreign countries.

PRESENTATION SKILLS

With so much training provided in recent years on presentation skills, it would seem a luxury to include the topic in a chapter on negotiation skills!

KEY TECHNIQUES: PRESENTATION SKILLS

Negotiation meetings require more economical and persuasive presentation skills and the following characteristics will be useful:

- ❑ Crisp presentation with minimal waffling.
- ❑ Presentation of the case 'sunny-side-up'.
- ❑ Sensitivity to the effects on the audience – by minimizing the use of provocative language and/or words with emotive effects (observation of body language will help with this).
- ❑ Avoiding too much minutiae – detail kills principles.
- ❑ Being economical with information presentation – without leaving the impression that specific information is being withheld.
- ❑ Aiming for maximum fluency.

The following chart illustrates the importance of presentation skills in negotiation

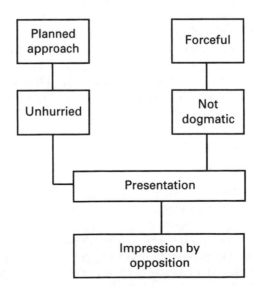

CASE HISTORY

A recently trained union convenor set about his first joint meeting with the local management team with great enthusiasm. Having established his role in speaking first he rose to his feet and regaled the assembled gathering with a 45-minute dissertation on the Tolpuddle martyrs! Apart from mild surprise from his opponents, he earned substantial loss of support (and most of his credibility), from his own team! Such 'own goals' are hardly desirable in negotiation presentations.

Effective negotiators observe the effects of their presentations on their opponents *and* their own teams – and seek to minimize any negative effects.

TEAM COMMUNICATIONS

One of the fascinating aspects of negotiation in teams is the whole process of communicating *inside the team*. We are all taught *not* to whisper in public (because it is thought to be rude) – but how else are we to communicate with our colleagues?

A related issue is the preparation of an appropriate seating plan – and its agreement inside the team. If it is unlikely that we are able to talk to each other in front of our opponents, then passing notes will be essential – as well as non-verbal signals such as eye contact, a raised eyebrow or even a nudge or a kick!

Certainly eye contact will be easier if the team leader is seated in the middle of his or her group, and the obvious grouping would enable eye contact to be 'caught' without attracting the attention of opponents.

In well-practised groups, some verbal codes may also be used to warn team members that they will be expected to support the leader in a few moments. For example, a union leader might say: 'I am glad that you brought up the question of shift payments because there are some pretty strong feelings around in the works about that [cue for the works convenor to fire a barrage]. I think you had something to say about that, Freda' (turns to the convenor and 'gives permission' to make her presentation). The 'ball' might then be returned, by request, when the leader says speedily: 'As you can see, feelings are running pretty strong in the factory and we would urge you to give careful consideration to these issues before they become *really* emotive.'

Few people would wish their notes to be read by their opponents and written codes have been known in highly competitive meetings (one team was trained to write in phonetic Greek so that their notes could not be read – even if anyone would want to). The danger with these 'games' is that they may assume an importance of their own and distract from the main purpose of the meeting.

CRITICAL BEHAVIOURS TO AVOID IN TEAM NEGOTIATION

Behaviours which are likely to prove counter-productive are:

- **Defence and attack** – provocation is best ignored and side-stepped.
- **Blocking** – reasoned disagreement is preferable as it keeps discussion flowing.
- **Argument dilution** – do not 'shoot yourself in the foot'.
- **Irritators** – create barriers in others and erode possible support.
- **Counter-proposals** – encourage competitive win/lose behaviour and outcomes. Any feeling of 'haggling' is best avoided in most business sectors.
- **Shutting out** (overtalking someone else) – is rude and contributes to heated emotions and possible conflict.
- **Disagreeing** – building on their proposals and moulding them towards your own objectives is the best way of persuading and encouraging change.

PROGRESS TOWARDS THE BETTER DEAL

Behaviours which will contribute to an effective meeting are:

- Making proposals and rewarding the proposals of others
- Building
- Supporting
- Testing understanding
- Seeking information
- Bringing in.

REVIEW ASSIGNMENT

With the agreement of the parties involved, observe the behaviours used in a team negotiation against the following list described above:

POSITIVE BEHAVIOURS

☐ Making proposals and
☐ Rewarding the proposals of others
☐ Building
☐ Supporting
☐ Testing understanding
☐ Seeking information
☐ Bringing in

NEGATIVE BEHAVIOURS

☐ Defence and attack
☐ Blocking
☐ Argument dilution
☐ Irritators
☐ Counter-proposals
☐ Shutting out (overtalking someone else)
☐ Disagreeing

If it is not possible to observe a team negotiation, the following plan would provide an alternative assignment. Seeking the prior approval of the parties involved, observe a one-to-one negotiation and try to record the number of times the above 'behaviours' are used by the two parties (using the above criteria). Then compare the results with data you or a colleague might collect on a similar project meeting (and the results you might have achieved).

Team negotiations are sometimes the cause of, and possibly an answer to, conflict situations. Chapter 9 provides an analysis on how to handle conflict.

9 *Conflict – and how to handle it*

INTRODUCTION

This chapter is about conflict – something which sadly often arises in negotiation meetings. Its inclusion in this book is designed to help the reader:

- research the root causes and 'politics' involved in conflict;
- consider the motivators of conflict; and
- identify causes of deadlock and how to resolve it.

Negotiators who have been closely involved in conflict tell of the strong impact it has had on them. The real risk is that these experiences colour their attitudes towards negotiation, generally – making it (perhaps) more difficult for collaborative bargaining techniques to be developed and applied.

Why does negotiation create so much conflict?

It clearly does, and no work on the subject would be complete without a section on how to handle it.

What are the roots of conflict?

Generally it occurs when both 'sides' want the same thing and cannot have it. Or, the two sides are exceptionally competitive and each sees the other as standing in the way of their goals. How can this arise? The competitive spirit may arise from:

- **Instinctive dislike** – the two parties 'rub each other up the wrong way from the start'.
- **Value-driven conflict** – there is a natural opposition between the characters born out of their different backgrounds and culture – e.g.: 'working class' versus 'privileged background'.
- **Materialistic or status needs** driven on one side versus security needs on the other.

■ The need to maintain a **personal reputation** and track record of 'success' (and the opponent is seen as an obstacle to the maintenance of this reputation).

The problem with each of these factors is that they contribute to the idea that negotiation is a 'zero-sum game'. In other words, the whole exercise can only result in a win/lose outcome. We know now, from earlier chapters, that this is not the case and that, with thorough preparation and determination, a larger, better deal can be obtained – representing a win/win. This is more likely when both sides *want* to achieve a better deal!

It is also possible that a negotiator's individual style provokes conflict – intentionally or not; readers may be able to identify negotiators they have met who use the approaches described in the next section and will clearly be best advised to prepare carefully before 'entering the ring'.

There is a risk that, unchecked – and without a considerable personal effort to prevent escalation – conflict can take the progressive form illustrated in the following diagram:

PERSECUTION COMPLEX

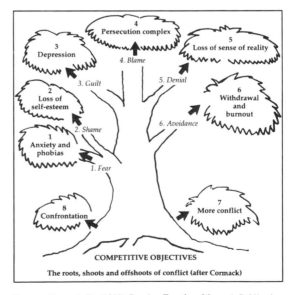

The roots, shoots and offshoots of conflict (after Cormack)

Source: Cormack, D. (1989) *Peacing Together*, Monarch Publications

RESEARCH THE 'POLITICS' BEHIND THE OTHER PARTY'S POSITION

As we saw at the beginning of this book, different people see negotiation in quite different ways. Broadly speaking, the more competitive they are at heart, the more likely they will be to adopt a competitive approach to a negotiation. For instance, they may see the process as akin to:

(a) **A 'race'** – only the winner will walk away with the gold medal and everything else is second best. (Often described as a 'zero-sum game' – and illustrated in the following diagram).

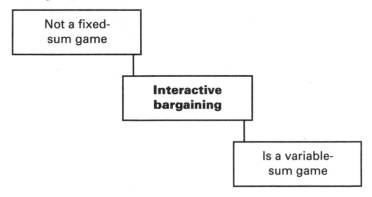

(b) An event in which the other party may be weakened by constant **'point-scoring'** – mainly done to impress an audience (usually the 'own side').

(c) **Bidding** – as at an auction – a process in which one customer is manipulated to believe that he or she is bidding for a deal against other unseen players.

(d) **Haggling** – just as if the product or service is being traded in a street market.

(e) Pressure to win, protect or gain **market share** or benefits for the consumer (this method drives many commercial bargains and can lead to over-preoccupation with price issues risking many other valuable goals to be overlooked).

(f) **'Arm-wrestling'** – an opportunity to boost one's ego by exhibiting power and strength – the principal aim being the subjugation of the opponent.

CASE HISTORY

The board of a major plc established a new trading policy incorporating new selling price levels and conditions of sale. The Sales Director met with three important clients who were incensed about the new policy but did not attempt to negotiate it out. Two of them complained about the attitude of the Sales Director direct to the MD who promptly took over relations with them directly and reversed the board decision (in their cases only). The Sales Director was excluded from all future negotiations with these customers.

The **processes** used by negotiators to resolve differences may also give an insight into their view of conflict. For example, some parties may be quick to resort to:

(a)   **Law** – where the 'best' (most expensive?) lawyer may stand a better chance of winning – leaving the opponent with a very public, and expensive, 'lose'.

CASE HISTORY

With the regulating authority's approval, a major insurance company (specializing in motor insurance) removed its operations from an EU country to an offshore-island location because of the favourable tax environment. Once it had established its operations at the new location, it became insolvent leaving all the policyholders exposed – and also the re-insurers. There was some suspicion that the move – and the liquidation – had been planned together to avoid additional losses/claims. The situation and legal responsibilities could only be resolved by the courts.

(b)   **Arbitration** – where the negotiator is convinced of the 'rightness' of his or her case and sees the *process of arbitration* as the means of achieving the goal.

(c)   **Pressure groups** – resorting to the media may buttress the case being pressed by a negotiator – for example, Greenpeace may generate considerable sympathy amongst non-supporters for particular ecological action and fight a case for the wider public good (even though their committed support may appear to be small in paid-up numbers). Their engagement of the media may bring about achievement of their objectives even when they are in a 'David and Goliath' struggle.

(d) **Taking 'hostages'** – this could include a unilateral decision to cut off communities by the withdrawal of transport services or perhaps the decision to build a bridge to replace a ferry – the cost of which has to be paid for with expensive toll fees. Negotiators will seek ways of ensuring that the 'aggressors' in such cases do not benefit from their actions.

(e) **'Honest broker'** – the party may seek a reputable body to act as mediator in cases of a struggle; the higher the perceived standing of the broker, the more likely the parties will be to present objective evidence, agree procedures and debate the issues.

CASE HISTORY

In the case of a software contract drafted between a public body and an independent computer consultancy, a method of resolving any disputes was written into the documents. Should any complaint remain unresolved, either party could call upon the current President of the British Computer Society to act as arbiter. (This 'safety net' was never exercised as there were no problems requiring this step.)

ASSIGNMENT 1

Given the above processes and methods of resolving conflict, analyse some examples of known disputes inside and outside your own organization:

INTERNAL

Situation	Process(es)	Resolution method

Then consider the following cases/personalities:

- The late Robert Maxwell when negotiating over a 'libel' case.
- Greenpeace and the Shell Oil company over the Brent Spar oil installation.
- The Skye bridge saga.
- The debate about banning handguns in the UK after the Hungerford and Dunblane tragedies.
- The Major government's tactics in seeking the EU to drop the ban on British beef following the BSE controversy.
- Establishment of the peace forum in Northern Ireland.

EXTERNAL

Situation	Process(es)	Resolution method

MOTIVATORS OF CONFLICT

Apart from the style factors considered above, conflict may be 'motivated' by fear, blackmail or a sense of fairness (misplaced or just):

(a) **Defeat or humiliation**. Negotiators or parties may feel obliged to 'fight' simply because they feel they have no option – they have been boxed in and the alternative to fighting is to accept conditions which will be perceived as a humiliating defeat. (This position can also lead to a damaging lose/lose where the pressurized party reclaims 'ownership of the ball and refuses to allow the game to continue'!).

CASE HISTORY

Divorce lawyers are sadly familiar with the use of false accusations made during the divorce proceedings. Where custody is in question, it is not unheard of that a child might be manipulated to make false sexual abuse accusations against a parent in an attempt to manipulate the outcome of the case. Desperate people sometimes take desperate measures.

(b) **Retaliation**. 'You did that to me – so I am doing this to you!' This sounds awfully like 'playground politics' and such tit-for-tat tactics can have a habit of getting out of hand.

(c) **Thin end of the wedge**. Where one party senses that pressure from the opponent represents a pressure which could quickly lead to a trend, they may feel more obliged to 'steel' themselves for a battle to dissuade other similar proposals being advanced (for example, the major industrial conflict against Eddie Shah and the *Messenger* newspaper).

CASE HISTORY

The enforced redundancy of a manager in a public body led him to retaliate by taking his former employer to an industrial tribunal. His case was that his contract was unexpired and that the remaining period should be compensated by the employer. The case turned on which was 'superior' – the contract terms or the redundancy – and the tribunal found in favour of the

> former employee in this case. The result was a substantial pay-off and a thorough re-examination by the employer of the whole employing process (from advertisement to contractual documents) to ensure that other cases did not follow (thin end of the wedge). In this instance, the legal interpretation was important – and could not have been negotiated out between the parties.

(d) **Deterrent**. Many high-profile disputes are kept in balance by the parties who fear that similar tactics may be adopted by their opponents with possible detrimental and unpredictable effects. This is sufficient to stop the use of that particular tactic. (For example, it is argued that owning weapons of mass destruction contributed to 40 years of peace between East and West – simply because neither side could realistically contemplate using them.)

(e) **Test of strength**. Sometimes a conflict might be a test of strength or willingness to 'fight' set up by a surrogate body – designed to expose the main party's tactics. For example, in international relations, the Cuban missile crisis might have been seen as the USSR's testing of the USA's resolve to prevent an expansion of nuclear potential on their own doorstep ('Cuba today, where tomorrow?').

(f) **Macho power**. Large is reckoned by most people to mean powerful – but how can this be demonstrated? An obvious way is by bullying other, smaller players in the market – competitors or even clients. So, a very large retailer might deliberately breach pricing protocols (e.g. recommended retail prices) as a competitive weapon, but also to flex its muscles on a much wider stage.

(g) **Guerrilla warfare**. In some forums, the desire to be destructive is much stronger than the desire to be constructive. This may not necessarily be an expression of hatred – just that the 'players' dislike the system so much that they are determined to change it for good! (It has been said that some communist cells have been motivated this way and the continuance of strike action after 'reasonable' compromises have been offered might be thought to be an indication of such tactics. Equally, an employer's determination to sack strikers who feel that they have a legitimate grievance might also create the impression that a reasonable solution is unlikely to placate both sides of the dispute.)

(h) **Levers**. These can provide highly effective means of obtaining a resolution of disputes, especially when one party is desperate to get on with, say, a major project. For example, a company anxious to establish a new, bipartisan forum for health and safety procedures covering its national operations may find itself held up by one of its employee representatives who is urgently seeking major change in one, small, local plant.

With this collection of 'motivators' it should also be remembered that conflict is often 'stoked up' by many observers, players, the media, and even individual citizens. Politicians sometimes find themselves looking over their shoulders and considering what public opinion makes of a particular issue – before becoming committed to positive courses of action. This concern sometimes motivates the behaviour of senior managers – in commercial markets, as well as industrial relations disputes. Many a macho manager – regularly using expletives to describe what he (or she) intends to do to the opponent – turns out to 'purr like a pussy cat' when in the privacy of the buyer's office. Such behaviour is intended to create an effect on the 'troops' but rarely cuts much ice once the individual's 'cover is blown'! However, until this day arrives perhaps all less experienced negotiators reporting to such a macho manager might model themselves on this type of behaviour. What could be the consequences of this?

So why else is conflict 'stoked-up'?

(a) **Enjoyment**. It has to be said that some people just love a row; a fight; the opportunity to prove themselves. Two young stags determined to fight the issues out until one party is exhausted or mortally wounded. (The dispute between the National Coal Board and the National Union of Mineworkers could be viewed in this way. The frightening factor is that *both sides* could have been described as losers in that dispute.)

(b) **Brinkmanship**. Unfortunately, the failure of any of the parties to prepare properly (and analyse the politics of the dispute as well as the facts), may simply create a determination to push the issues right to the brink of a major conflict. In other words the determination to keep fighting becomes greater than any perceived advantages to be gained from resolving the conflict. Unfortunately, the players may lose sight of what is a realistic goal – one which is really attainable. This can sometimes lead to complete reversals of win/lose deals; a macho player manipulates a contractor into believing that he cannot afford *not* to win the contract and finally obtains a very one-sided deal – only to have the contractor liquidate when it is too late to have another party take over the contract and still achieve that publicly quoted opening date!

(c) **False expectations**. Inexperienced negotiators may be lured into believing that they can obtain deals well below (or above) market price after hearing in a bar somewhere of the other party's conquests. This might lead them to hold out for unrealistic deals which may only be attainable against some hidden agenda of motives on the other side. (For example, double glazing that is so far below market value that the deal is only possible with inferior materials and this leads to an expensive and protracted dispute between the parties which makes the whole experience one best forgotten!)

It has to be said that, in all disputes 'right' is rarely totally on one side rather than the other and, even when it is, obtaining a declaration to that effect may not resolve the problem. Resorting to warfare, for example, may satisfy the 'hawks' in a dispute but, long after casualties have been incurred on both sides, someone has to build a vision of a just peace which the combatants can live with. Alternatives to this lead to yet more dangerous and costly disputes in the future (it is one thing to declare war and quite another to get it put back in the 'box' with the lid screwed down tightly).

So, for matters of principle, the parties may risk life, limb, reputations and perhaps substantial amounts of money to be proved 'right'. The costs of resolving the conflict *before it comes to a head* may turn out to be a great deal less than the costs involved in the fight!

DEADLOCK

Two senior negotiators, when called upon to negotiate out a team exercise, found themselves unable to reach agreement on the values they placed on various techniques they used. The whole debate ultimately faltered on the need to 'avoid deadlock at all costs'. One party felt that, in his industry, it was totally unrealistic to 'throw £50 notes at the situation just to avoid deadlock'! The other emphasized that, in his experience, time means money and that, whilst he could conceive situations where stalemates could occur, deadlock simply protracted negotiation and increased the attendant costs – a definite no/no in his highly profitable enterprise. This highly pragmatic approach should be remembered, of course, when matters of principle are involved – is it better to take 'the hit' now and get on with the next deal which should be much better (and profitable) rather than waste time arguing about this one?

So, identifying the issues which may become deal-busters are important in any negotiation. This step should be an integral part of the discussion and proposal phases. The reluctance of the opponent to move on a particular issue – even when concessions or inducements are offered – may cause the spectre of a no-deal stalemate to arise.

It is easy to visualize a determined, extrovert negotiator set about such an obstacle like an archetypal, pushy salesperson and become quite incensed when 'reason' supports the strength of his arguments but the opponent simply digs in with even more determination. (Remember the 'Niet, Niet, Niet' example of Mr Khrushchev's shoe-banging at the United Nations referred to in chapter 4.)

There is a danger that such tactics on both sides may lead to conflict – the irresistible force and the immovable object – and complete deadlock. In commercial situations, there may be good reasons why the deal *should be progressed*. Logic may dictate that so much money has already been invested in that new, but incomplete, computer system that it would be wrong to cancel the project now. However, what is there to stop a repeat over-run in the budget being presented by the supplier next year, if we have agreed to pay the unexpected excess this year?

In diplomatic terms, the overriding objective of maintaining peace by facing down the Cuban missile crisis may have led the world's heartbeat to falter for what seemed like interminable hours – but, in retrospect, peace was the winner!

In both situations, the **Best Alternative to a Negotiated Settlement (BATNeS)** may hardly seem to present a desirable way out. Resorting to force or the international court may not be very attractive either (just think of the delays and the legal costs). So, conflict resolution needs to be given careful consideration.

ASSIGNMENT 2

Perhaps an important starting-point is to consider how you felt when caught up in some position of deadlock. Were you:

❑   Self-righteous?
❑   Frustrated? Angry? (Especially if you felt they denied you a 'win'.)
❑   Irritated by the potential loss of face, time, money, effort etc.?
❑   Allocating blame to your opponent?
❑   Seeking retribution from your opponents?

What did you learn from the situation – and the experience?

Hopefully the situation should *and could* have been avoided with a little more patience and care. Here are some of the factors which can help break a deadlock.

DEADLOCK AND CONFLICT RESOLUTION

Here are some ways of defusing conflict in negotiation meetings with the objective of achieving consensus and a win/win deal! We will consider:

■   ignoring the conflict by focusing on objectives;
■   smoothing things over;
■   withdrawal of one (or both!) of the parties;
■   resolution by working it through;
■   arbitration by a third party;

before approaching the finishing stages of the negotiation.

Focus on objectives

As we have seen, conflicting behaviour and attitudes in meetings can provide very effective distractions from the main business in hand – which is scary! It might be thought of as 'fun' – or even tactical – to provoke the opponent but this may turn out to be a wasteful game if it results in deadlock. Both sides need to meet the objectives of the meeting (unless one party has a clear intention of a lose/lose result – and if this is the case it should have been identified in their opponent's preparation). Focusing on the goals to be achieved – and the benefits to be gained – may help to restore a level of *motivation* and *intention* to reach agreement where these factors had been eroded before.

Smoothing

Diplomats are past masters at smoothing over difficulties. All their years of training have helped them smooth over even aggressive situations as 'little local difficulties' and, even when their 'masters' have fallen out, they try to maintain the closest of relationships with their opposite numbers at the local level. This is what they are paid to do – and more often than not, it works!

Conciliation services try to focus on the same role. For example, the marriage guidance counsellor may try to help the parties to express, and then resolve, their disputes and difficulties by smoothing out the emotions and aggression in favour of the greater objective. A highly skilled diplomat or conciliator will make conflict and disagreement sound like agreement all round!

Withdrawal

Once the full impact of the possibilities resulting from deadlock or conflict becomes clear, one of the parties may draw back from their position – enabling some further *exchange of concessions* (this will work well where they can be convinced that their opponent will not simply move on to a further demand). In other words, recognition of the greater 'public good – or issues' may motivate the parties to 'sink their differences'.

Withdrawal of one party (by recess) may enable a period of reflection to take place on both sides. Trying to be objective about the situation may still defeat highly emotional negotiators – and the only way in which progress may be made could be to replace the negotiators themselves!

Resolution

Conflict resolution is not always a pretty sight. Macho negotiators have been known to threaten opponents in meetings with intimidating behaviour (e.g. rolling up sleeves in threatening ways) and, sadly, it is not unknown for such situations to lead to a 'punch-up' in some back alley. Managers can be just as guilty – and, whilst 'fisticuffs' may be the ultimate in aggressive behaviour, some people find a really good row very satisfying in itself. Expressing innermost feelings in an unrestrained way (what politicians might call a 'robust discussion') at least lets all the parties know where they stand. The dangers are obvious. In the general melée, things may be said from which there can be no easy apology and bruised egos simply result in an increasing determination that the opponents will *not be allowed to succeed*. Once again commitment to ultimate agreement needs to be paramount to make such tactics successful.

CASE HISTORY

Social workers sometimes feel themselves to be in a no-win situation. In child protection cases, if they are too relaxed the life of the child may be at stake; too tough and they may be accused of over-reaction. However, they have considerable flexibility over their negotiating style – always with the objective of defending the child's best interests. In Emergency Protection Order cases, a social worker may feel obliged to present the case in a macho way to gain co-operation from parents. For example: 'A statutory body has to make its intentions clear to the parties involved; we believe this child to be at risk and it is our intention to seek a court order for the fostering of the child.' Such a powerful presentation may be adopted in order to obtain the co-operation of the parents with the processes which will follow. The stakes are high and misreading the situation could result in tragedies such as those played out in the Orkneys and the late Kimberley Carlile.

Arbitration

In the precise sense of the word, an arbitrator could be described as a go-between – a counsellor who seeks to advise both parties on their dispute, encourage objective thought and so suggest solutions which will suit both sides. Sometimes, the arbiter is needed because the two sides have lost complete control and cannot bear to think of themselves having to share the same room as the other party! So, the conciliator becomes the 'mouthpiece' or 'conduit' for the two sides.

However, the process of arbitration really goes further than this – some guarantee must be provided that *both sides* (or all parties) will agree to implement the decisions of the arbiter – or there is no point in going to arbitration in the first place. Arbitration is not an automatic method of resolving conflict unless the parties agree to this in advance – and, ideally, there should be some legal frame-work or sanctions made to apply if the final settlement is not supported.

ASSIGNMENT 3

Following Iraq's invasion of Kuwait, consider the methods which were used by the Western allies to persuade the aggressors to leave – and then the methods used to ensure that the invasion was most unlikely ever to be repeated.

BEHAVIOURS TO AVOID IF CONFLICT SITUATIONS ARE TO BE MINIMIZED

Skilled and experienced negotiators try to avoid manipulating their opponents if they believe that this will lead to conflict – and a lose/lose result. Specific behaviours to be avoided are:

- **Counter-proposals** – deliberately adopting a haggling style.
- **Irritators** – where one party deliberately uses verbal, or non-verbal, behaviour to 'wind-up' the opponent(s) – which may result in an emotional outburst (it is then argued that the instigators of the 'irritants' can grasp the high moral ground by making it seem that *they* are the responsible, reliable, emotionally mature 'players' who have the *real interests of the company/state/union/manufacturing plant (etc.) at heart*!
- **Argument dilution** is a self-induced 'goal' which is created by mixing sound and weak arguments in support of a case. The mistake lies in listing all these points together so that the opponent may

choose a weak one to explode, followed by another, and another – leaving probably the only sound argument exposed to a belittling process and creating a 'moral victory' because all the other issues were proved to be worthless! If experienced negotiators avoid falling into this trap, what should be done when the opponent seems to have perpetuated this fault (perhaps through naïveté)? The true diplomat would certainly try to avoid creating negative reactions by climbing up the weak argument ladder before issuing the *coup de grâce*! Given the probability that the behaviour is an indication of inexperience, the skilled player will not worry about addressing the weak arguments but simply address the one or two strong ones.

■ **Defence and attack behaviours** can provoke playground warfare which can easily get out of hand. Skilled negotiators do all that they can to ignore and avoid reacting to the emotional overtones used in these behaviours. This may be easier said than done! Counting to ten before responding may be a valuable way of ensuring that the negotiator thinks before acting – or speaking – but the hurt of an unjust accusation or downright lie may be too much to ignore. As we have seen, little is really gained by an irrational discussion – or even an absolute row. Things may be said – accusation, followed by counter-accusation – that would be much better unsaid if persuasion is to be effective. There is probably no jury to convince, no judge or procedure to hold the balance – only a fast-declining prospect of persuading the opposition to agree! *So, don't be tempted*!

If or when an attack spirals out of control and leads to verbal abuse, take a mental side-step and allow the 'arrows' to fly over your shoulder, keeping cool and showing that you have no intention to join in the 'game'. A recess will also help to calm emotions and tempers.

■ **Blocking** is another behaviour to avoid in such situations – objecting to proposals without any supporting reasons can be annoying in the extreme and contribute to the creation of a conflict. Sweet reason is the rock on which logical debate is founded and negotiation will be much more likely to fail when reason is absent.

■ **Psychological pressures and games** can also contribute to emotional situations, deadlock and even conflict and are not normally used by skilled negotiators. Such pressures as:

❏ Taking the **higher seat** (whilst the opponent has the lower one).

- ❏ Deliberately **facing the opponent into the light** so that he or she finds it difficult to focus on facial expression and eye contact.
- ❏ Adopting a **low reactor** style of interaction (i.e. deliberately not saying very much) can also be extremely intimidating – especially for a natural extrovert (naïve extroverts may not even notice this happening).
- ❏ Imposing a completely **unrealistic timescale** on the meeting and then calling 'time-out' before the opponent has had a reasonable chance to present a case also throws serious doubts on the party's intentions to reach anything other than an imposed solution in the first instance.
- ❏ Doing everything possible to **shut-out** the opponent (perhaps by overtalking or constantly interrupting).

Readers will doubtless be able to recall opponents they have met who have tried various of these tactics – and may have even tried some of them, too! There is little doubt that, in subtle ways, they can be made to work – but what kind of reaction is likely to be forthcoming if they are unsubtle, and simply attract ridicule from the opponent? Who is likely to feel at an advantage then?

TOWARDS THE BETTER DEAL

As we have seen, conflict can be a natural element in negotiations – especially when the parties feel they are in competitive situations. The obvious motive is for both parties to try to focus on the big issues, the 'grand design', the overall objectives – and avoid precipitate action or behaviour which may simply provoke conflagration. Skilled negotiators maintain as much reasonableness in their debate by using:

- ■ **Proposals** rather than counter-proposals.
- ■ **Building** behaviour to add to or change their opponent's proposals (making it appear that it was 'their' idea all along).
- ■ **Seeking information** behaviour (especially open questions) rather than imposing a fog with a myriad of facts, information and opinion.
- ■ **Clarifying behaviours** – especially through **testing** their own **understanding** of what has been said, and **summarizing**.

■ **Giving support/agreement**, where possible – and praising offers and welcoming ideas (which helps to motivate more of them).
■ **Labelling behaviour** before it is used (e.g. 'May I just ask a question?) which helps to gain the other party's attention.
■ **Bringing the other person in** (e.g. 'I am sure you have some views on that idea.').

Finally, a most powerful tactic – but one which should not be over-used for fear of it losing its effect – is the sharing or revealing of **inner feelings**. If negotiation is about persuading other parties to move towards the position you desire, such a result is hardly likely if they are feeling angry, upset or frustrated with you or your organization. A 'poker face' and masterly self-control may conceal these feelings and so revealing them in a simple sentence can have an awesome effect! Again, understatement may have much more effect than an emotional outburst and still enable the 'players' to focus on the ultimate goal – a freely entered into deal which benefits both sides and can be readily implemented; in other words, the topic of chapter 10!

REVIEW ASSIGNMENT

Continuing with the observation assignments described in chapter 8 – and choosing a situation which may involve some conflict – a useful assignment would be to observe and analyse the behaviours used from the following table:

■ **Counter-proposals**
■ **Irritators**
■ **Argument dilution**
■ **Defence and attack behaviours**
■ **Blocking**
■ **Psychological pressures and games**
  ❏ Taking the **higher seat**
  ❏ Deliberately **facing the opponent into the light**
  ❏ Adopting a **low reactor** style of interaction
  ❏ Imposing completely **unrealistic timescales**
  ❏ **Shut-outs**.

---

10 Closing the negotiation

INTRODUCTION

There is always a danger that, with the finishing line in view, the racing driver makes a mistake, loses concentration, or fails to notice a fellow competitor sneaking up on the inside! Negotiation can be an exciting activity since it is nearly always about some future plan, scheme or facility. The sudden realization that plans that were laid weeks and weeks ago will actually come to fruition *is* exciting in itself. However, many a slip can still occur in the closing stages and, just like the racing driver who has the race snatched from his grasp in the closing seconds, negotiators have been known to rue the day they ever invented the plan in the first place – through some omission, error of judgement or forlorn hope – which worms its way into the deal and dilutes its effectiveness or value.

In this chapter we will consider ways of closing the meeting and applying the skills often normally associated with salespeople:

- building and maintaining relationships;
- recognizing obstacles to the deal through careful probing;
- applying some specific closing techniques (and avoiding others!);
- avoiding the temptation of greed;

as well as describing some behaviours which will pay for themselves over and over, and some potential 'traps' to avoid.

CLOSING SKILLS

Building and maintaining relationships

There is little doubt that one of the most important skills or senses for the negotiator to develop is that of good timing. Some meetings can go round and round in circles – just begging for one of the parties to close them up. Equally, the really extrovert salesperson may have some unpleasant experiences when seeking agreement of a deal through trying to close prematurely and perhaps even putting the client off for good! In all win/win deals where the development and enhancement of goodwill is a main objective, the maintenance and development of good relationships is crucial. So, the closing stage needs to be handled confidently – but also sensitively.

ASSIGNMENT 1: SURVEY ON CLOSING

A real challenge for negotiators is choosing the right moment for the closing process. All sellers and buyers have experienced meetings which have stalled, taken twice as long as they might have done or have closed prematurely. With the objective of learning from others, complete a short survey of colleagues to draw out their experiences of closing:

Stalled meetings
❏ Have they experienced meetings that have stalled?
❏ What caused this?
❏ What could they have done about it? Was a settlement possible?
❏ How were relationships affected?

Long-winded meetings
❏ Which meetings they have attended that were unduly lengthy? What caused this?
❏ What could they have done about it? Which closing methods did they try? With what result?
❏ How were relationships affected?

Premature closes
❏ Which meetings closed prematurely? Why did it happen?
❏ What effect, if any, did this have on the final deal?
❏ How were relationships affected?

These experiences should provide a helpful base for comparison with the techniques described later in this chapter.

Recognizing obstacles to the deal through careful probing

Here we are, right at the end of the storyline, proposals have been exchanged and, broadly, agreed but still your opponent has not actually said 'Yes'! Does he or she need to? What is wrong with the implied close – all the signals seem to be at green but not one concrete affirmation has been uttered!

What are the options? Clearly, asking for the deal would be a positive move – as most sales training manuals state: 'So, Mrs Jones, may I have your agreement to go ahead with this order with your signature on the order form?'

Many salespeople baulk at asking this question – simply because it is a closed question and risks the 'No!' answer. Actually, unless the timing is much too early, or there are some outstanding issues which have not yet been sorted out, the other party will probably agree. If a 'Yes' is not given, the simple recovery is to try to discover the underlying reason(s) for withholding agreement. Something like: 'Oh, I'm sorry, there must be something I failed to cover – if you tell me what it is, I'm sure we can clear it up.'

It would, of course, be much better if this kind of issue does not arise – and one way of avoiding it is to build progress checks along the way in the meeting. For example: 'How do you feel about that?' or 'Was that the kind of scheme you were hoping for?' 'Have I been covering the kind of issue that you wanted clarifying?' 'Are you feeling that we might be close to reaching agreement now?'

Such progress checks are especially valuable when they seek the other party's *feelings* – since feelings may not be readily disclosed and yet they do provide a valuable indicator of progress to the ultimate goal. An answer like: 'Well, I was feeling rather unsure about the costs of servicing, but now you have explained the service intervals and the advantages of the extended warranty, I am feeling a lot more comfortable.' might easily lead to a final check: 'So, are there any other outstanding concerns that I haven't dealt with?'

If the answer to this question is 'No' then the meeting should be closed before any other doubts are created! The point here is that we should be sensitive to the needs and concerns of the other party – especially if we want more business from the client (or a continuing relationship with the supplier)!

CASE HISTORY

A person who was about to open a new business responded to a local advertisement for an essential business machine. The visiting representative booked the call and was only able to bring a brochure of the machine since 'all machines were out on demonstration'. After some time in discussing the technical features of the machine, the customer felt sufficiently confident about the specification and placed the order by signing the order form. He did not even worry about the quoted six-week lead-time for the machines to arrive at the dealership and was even prepared to write a cheque for the whole amount (including the VAT). However, the representative's manner changed after receiving the form and the cheque and left with considerable haste – promising to put a detailed invoice in the post! The businessman now had serious doubts about the wisdom of the deal and very nearly stopped the cheque. Actually, no problems ensued – the invoice arrived two days later (and the machine four weeks after that) but the undue haste had certainly projected unhelpful 'vibrations' which could easily have disturbed the customer's apparent commitment!

Negotiators are sometimes faced with a sudden change of heart in a meeting, such as: 'What on earth will my boss say about this? I know it is the best deal I can get, but I am already over-spent and we were all warned not to do it again by the Finance Director. Perhaps I had better think about it again and get my boss's approval in writing, before making a firm commitment!'

When on the receiving end of these 'thoughts' the opponent may have the firm feeling that the meeting is going to end in stalemate – and no committed deal. So, here is another instance where probing skills may:

■ reveal the problem;
■ invite a solution, such as staged payments.

Similarly, reluctance to close may arise from some inhibitions of the other party. Perhaps the 'best' offer on the table will not match the known expectations of the other party's boss. There is no argument that it seems to be fair – but the other party risks being castigated as a 'wimp' at the next management meeting unless something better is agreed. If these inhibitions are not expressed – and then addressed – the deal may still founder and a more sympathetic supplier/client sought!

Applying some specific closing techniques (and avoiding others!)

Those sales training manuals we mentioned above often give the impression that all the initiative (and action) will come from the sales side. This need not be the case; there is no reason why a deal or settlement should not be closed by the buyer – or the trade union (staff side) – even if this is not quite the 'textbook' way.

The only issue to consider is 'custom and practice'. If, for example, the act of closing is *always* the province of one side rather than the other, a unilateral step to change this could create suspicion in the other side – and possible protraction of the closing phase in case a trap has been laid! Specific closing techniques (in order of value in negotiation meetings) are:

- **The 'final' summary** – skilled negotiators summarize far more than average ones because they know that such clarifying behaviour builds up the other party's trust. Often, the final summary leads directly to the close and any 'asking for the deal' behaviour is quite unnecessary.
- **A final concession** – negotiators will sometimes try to motivate progress over the 'finishing line' by offering some small, final concession which will only be available if the deal is settled quickly. The illusion may be given that this extra offer is special – and certainly not available to everyone! There is nothing wrong in accepting this – but it should always be borne in mind that such inducements will have been costed into the package and that if the 'buyer' had negotiated a better deal then the supplier should not have been able to afford such last-minute offers! Indeed, there may be some more concessions forthcoming if a non-committal response is given.
- **The either/or, implied close** – is frequently used in shorter sales meetings and such an approach aims to avoid the use of the direct question: 'Now you seem happy with the model with the larger

engine and the de luxe trim, which colour shall we put you down for – the blue or the red?'

What is not on offer is the option not to decide today! Again, sensitive timing will enable the strong-willed negotiator to take the lead and 'help' the opponent to the final decision. 'After all, some people will never take a decision,' we might hear the car sales negotiator say!

■ **The recess** – is a rather more relaxed, soft-sell option and valuable when the negotiator senses that the opponent needs to be able to sell the deal to himself. In cases where the opponent really needs hand-holding, a recess could be dangerous – unless the uncertain party has some positive supporter(s) who are likely to be arguing for acceptance. Even so, an informal recess where one party gives the opponent space – but remains within earshot and possible eye contact – will enable supportive intervention without a feeling of 'pushiness'.

■ **The 'pull-out'** – is a real test of the opponent's commitment and might involve the quoting of an impending appointment which must be kept (real or invented) thus creating the need to fix another meeting to close the deal. Such 'crowding' techniques can have the reverse effect from that intended if the bluff is called and the option of a further date is supported. On the other hand, if commitment is high, the effect of this 'nudge' may be to move the meeting towards:

❑   one last summary and the close, or
❑   an alternative 'final offer' in which a sticking-point is compromised and an alternative close offered.

BEHAVIOURS BEST AVOIDED

Skilled negotiators who are concerned to achieve *better deals*, resist the temptation to:

Mis-summarize

This can be deliberate or unintentional but the effect is the same – the creation of agreement based on a false understanding of points said or 'agreed' so far. The test lies in the opponent's listening and the problem arises if the error goes unnoticed. It is much, much more difficult to change a summary later on if the earlier ones contain a mistake – and such a situation can quickly lead to recriminations and even conflict. Needless to say, the 'mis-summarizing' party is the one which is likely to express most annoyance: 'What is the point in us spending all this time in this meeting discussing these issues when you *now* say you never agreed to those early proposals? I have summarized all the areas of agreement as we have gone along, and *now* you tell me that you *don't agree them – never agreed them*, in fact! I'm sorry but it seems to me that we are wasting time here!'

Negotiators on the receiving end of this kind of attack should stand their ground if they feel that they are being pressurized or coerced into agreeing. BATNeS should always be an alternative option and may seem increasingly attractive in the face of this tactic.

Imposing unilateral deadlines

A famous historian stated that there never was a deadline in history that wasn't negotiable – and this is worth remembering when your opponent tries to pressurize with an impending price rise which 'could be avoided with a substantial order placed today'! What is being offered is just the same as what was offered last week/month/season and who is to say that substantial monies invested in *this product* will bring faster sales and quicker profits (over other propositions)? This does not mean that successful negotiators deliberately drag their feet either – realistic timing of any deal will depend most on the aspirations and protocols of either of the parties involved. What is needed is open, clear communication about what might be possible within realistic constraints.

All this is logical and cerebral thinking – but not always so achievable in real life when there are so many other pressures and deadlines. Communications are nearly always the function to suffer first, and so easily blamed when things go wrong resulting in a potential deal being ignored or overlooked.

Skilled negotiators manage to maintain an exquisite sense of timing – and are *not* constantly relying on the other party to 'pull the chestnuts out of the fire'!

Close in one 'leap'

Consider this position: it is 10.00am and your Divisional Director calls for you to go to his office for an urgent meeting. In five minutes flat, he explains that the organization needs you to go immediately to see an important client in the Far East (the round trip/project will take three weeks) and hands you plane tickets for a flight leaving in four hours' time. All the reasoning is plausible and, with your mind in a turmoil, you return to your office, with thoughts about how to tell your family, the location of your passport and what you need to take – completely forgetting about the immediate meeting in which you have to close negotiations on an important deal you have been working on for several weeks – with a new, external organization.

When the other party arrives, in a few minutes' time, he or she quickily recognizes that your priorities have changed and, having caught up with the problem, leads into a parallel story about having to drive straight off to Inverness for an urgent meeting: 'What has gone wrong with this crazy world?'

After some joint commiserations, your visitor sympathizes that time will be quite hard to find now for the full meeting you had both planned but wonders if, after all the time spent in discussions up to now, whether your positions can really be that far apart? After a little more sympathizing he suggests that, if you are able to put forward your best position, he will do whatever he can to match it. Would you:

(a)   Refuse politely and dash for the plane (picking up the loose end on your return)?
(b)   Tell him your best position and see if he can match it?
(c)   Refuse politely but make an alternative appointment for the week of your return?

If you chose option (b), what could possibly be wrong with this? You have been working on the project together for some time, the overall relationship seems healthy, collaborative, trusting etc. and you will need each other through the period of implementation . . . what could be wrong?

Playing devil's advocate, who is to say there really is an urgent trip planned for Inverness? Who says that your 'best offer or position' is really matched by his? The plausible urgency of the situation has negated the opportunity for the two parties to test out each other's positions – and there is a risk that the final deal will benefit your opponent much more than you!

On the other hand, all your researches and preparation shows that he (and his organization) has a thoroughly trustworthy reputation and that there is much to be said for being decisive and moving this deal forward.

As stated, skilled negotiators avoid these pressures if at all possible – it is best *not* to try to close a negotiation in one leap – even though it might make you feel good!

Fall prey to greed!

Greedy people usually get found out eventually – their greed gets the better of them. Negotiating from a position of trust may be tested should your opponent make a genuine mistake during the bargaining process. Such an event could create various reactions:

- If it was a genuine error, should we tell them?
- Did they mean it? Was there an ulterior motive? (That is, could it be a test of *our integrity*?)
- Should we ignore it and carry on as if we had not spotted the error? (Would they tell us if we made a similar error?)
- What could happen some time from now if or when they discover their mistake?
- How should we point out the error? (Without destroying their credibility.)

Is there a 'right' answer to these questions?

At seminars, we often discuss the maxim that perhaps it would be nice 'for us to do unto others that which we would hope they might do unto us' in similar circumstances! Anyway, with the mistake included, would the agreement be viable? Would the other parties look for some ways in which it might prove unworkable/unenforceable – even leading to public recriminations (and possible legal action). It might be 'fun' to develop the image of being a 'sharp operator' but, when integrity is missing, the lack of long-term trust can be the beginning of the end for a greedy negotiators' operations!

ASSIGNMENT 2: SURVEY OF BEHAVIOURS BEST AVOIDED

Using a different audience, complete a survey of negotiators to check on their experiences of the following behaviours/ techniques:

❑   Mis-summaries
❑   Unilateral deadlines
❑   Closing in 'one leap'
❑   Greed.

What were their reactions to these 'techniques' – how did they resist them?

If they did not notice the behaviours used at the time, what was their reaction when they realized what had happened?

If they resisted the behaviour at the time, how did they do it? And what was the effect on the deal? And the relationships with others at the meeting?

TOWARDS THE BETTER DEAL

The following checklist may help the reader avoid some of the most common mistakes:

(a)   before stating your 'final' agreement – summarize (or ask your opponent to do this); then:
(b)   listen very carefully;
(c)   check the summary against your objectives/notes;
(d)   ensure that all concessions are incorporated from *both sides*;
(e)   ask for it in writing – and compare *their* notes with *your* notes;
(f)   if legal checks have to be made, say so and agree a timetable;
(g)   ensure that all loose ends have been tied up – 'who is going to do what to whom' – especially apparently 'simple' factors such as 'terms and conditions of payment';
(h)   resurrect any earlier issues on which movement was not forthcoming;
(i)   obtain a commitment to the written confirmation of the deal.

The concluding process is illustrated in the following diagram which emphasizes the importance of ensuring that the deal is properly (and completely) recorded. Implementation problems will be more easily avoided if this were always carried out!

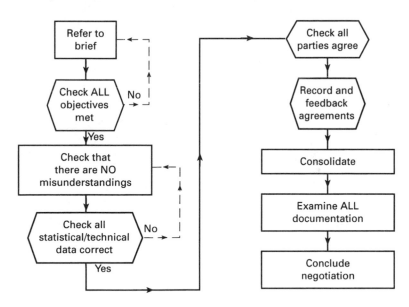

After all this has been followed, it might be time to celebrate – but don't forget that all the hard work you have contributed is now going to be thoroughly tested by reality – the implementation stage. Chapter 11 will help the reader through some of the key factors.

11 Implementing the deal

INTRODUCTION

This chapter is dedicated to considering ways of avoiding some of the more obvious (and costly) mistakes arising from a negotiation. It is a 'fraud'! It should not exist – because, by following the advice of earlier chapters, the reader should not be obliged to look for difficulties, or the ways in which an agreed deal may falter.

However, the unfortunate fact is that many deals do go wrong – for predictable, as well as unforeseeable, reasons and some people seem to spend most of their time negotiating their way out of one set of difficulties and straight into the arms of another set!

ASSIGNMENT 1: NEGOTIATING 'REARGUARD' ACTIONS

If this is you, perhaps you should stop and ask yourself a few questions:

❑   Do I prefer this way of life?
❑   Does 'sorting out problems/crises' make me feel good?
❑   If so, are any of the problems repeating? Self-made? Predictable?
❑   What do others make of all this? Am I developing a reputation as a 'fixer' or are people secretly amused/irritated by the tag 'busy fool'?
❑   Is 'crisis management' designed into the job I do? If so, can I influence other people to find better ways of using time and resources?
❑   If I want to use my resources to better effect – am I *really* applying the 'lessons' of this text as thoroughly as I ought?
❑   If this would be difficult for me to achieve, working on my own, whose help and support could I enlist?

> When you have considered these issues, compare them with the responses of another negotiator in your organization (perhaps your manager and a negotiator from a totally different discipline). Consider to what extent rearguard negotiating is endemic in your roles and/or the nature of your organization (and the market itself). Is there a better way?

The implementation of the agreement (and what can go wrong!) is the most important part of the whole process but one which properly belongs in a separate work altogether! 'Bloomers' exist in every walk of life and organization, and it is all negotiators' wish that their name is not attached to any of them. However, we have all made mistakes and the worst one of all is to *keep making the same mistakes*! Awareness of this dimension can help to avoid mistakes in the closing stages of the negotiation meeting and, sadly, too many negotiators learn these lessons the hard way! Protection against failures to implement include:

- accurate and detailed notes/agreed summaries;
- definitions of who will do what to/for whom and for what benefit or cost;
- consideration of what can go wrong (what if? analysis);
- how enforceable the agreement may be;

and we will close with some of the typical incidents which occur and which may reveal 'substandard' settlements arising from poor deals – a kind of 'rogues' gallery of deals'!

NOTES AND SUMMARIES

With photocopiers so readily at hand, there should be no reason why each negotiator should not have a detailed set of notes taken at each meeting. It is unfortunately quite common that we hear one thing at a meeting but write down something else! Mostly this is through wishful thinking or perhaps faulty listening – but how are such discrepancies viewed on the other side when they are eventually discovered? There is no quicker way of leading others to suspect your intentions, or even integrity! In some circles a buyer will insist on an exchange of notes before the representative leaves the buying room and these documents will probably form the basis of the ultimate order placed.

Even in such cases, the choices may be difficult to recall after the interview/show or trade mission; so, material samples are sought – and maybe Polaroid photographs taken. In very large-range plans, it can be difficult to recall, some weeks later, the precise colour or style of an item which may just be identified on the order form by a product code.

If the product fails to match the sample, when deliveries are made, a clearer case can be made for a credit if the true facts are recorded.

ASSIGNMENT 2

Compare notes with a representative group of negotiators in your organization – and compare their 'note-taking' habits. How many of them complete notes *after* the meeting (as opposed to *during* the meeting) and how long afterwards?

Does anyone actually record their meetings (with a pocket memo)? How was this agreed with the other party/ies?

If 'communiqués' have to be agreed for issue after a meeting, how are these agreed? Who issues them? What can go wrong? And how could it be put right or avoided?

LEVELS OF DETAIL

Disputes sadly occur at later dates about 'who-said-what-to-whom'! Rarely are negotiation meetings recorded (they may indicate a real lack of trust where they are); however, language in the meeting may well turn out to be ambiguous when it comes to implementation. Examples of expressions to be avoided include:

- 'As soon as possible' – this may indicate high levels of urgency to the sender, but the opposite to the receiver(!) – a precise date would be much better.
- 'The usual size scale' – whose? Ours? Yours? Someone else's? If such references are to be made then they should be attached/in writing/copied to all parties etc.

■ 'In the popular colours' – whose interpretation of popularity? Local? Regional? National? International? All colours will not be equally popular, so shouldn't the buyer specify precisely what he wants? Of course!

It is amazing just how many specification issues are overlooked in commercial negotiating – especially where a price-sensitive market is involved. For example, building-blocks may well be available at a substantial discount from those 'standard' units being supplied by the regular supplier. But do they do the same job? Is their insulation value the same? Maybe not; but the buyer might not care! Some months later the new house owner is wondering why his heating bills are so high and, if moved to investigate, may discover the truth!

WHAT IF?

What if there is a docks strike and we cannot obtain the product when we need it? Have we covered ourselves against consequential loss and would there be alternative supply points in such situations? What if there are substantial foreign exchange fluctuations and the currency markets move strongly against imported goods and services? Will we still be able to sell these products at a premium? What could go wrong?

Obviously, too many concerns of this type could provide serious disincentives to the deal at all. However, some contingency planning should be considered – and maybe some protection built into the contract (or covered by insurance). The last step will probably to go to court over some consequential loss – but without any clause in the contract, the negotiator may not even have his telephone or fax messages acknowledged (let alone answered!).

ENFORCEABILITY

We have all heard of negotiators who thought they had the contract nicely tied up – only to discover that some vital element is missing. Plain contracts are always preferable as disputes are usually simpler to negotiate than complex ones. Ultimately, if both sides wish to *continue to work together*, then negotiating a mutually acceptable solution to a dispute will be much easier without a huge entourage of specialists, accountants, lawyers etc. However, the bigger the issue (and sums involved), the more likely it is that the negotiators will need professional support and advice and, in such circumstances, progress may be tediously slow.

One of the objectives of the UK's industrial relations (IR) legislation in the 1980s was to make IR agreements more enforceable. The problem with this is that trade unions are democratic organizations – they cannot impose a view upon the membership – still less police the agreement. A number of disputes have arisen in that time where negotiated agreements – between management and union representatives – were then disowned by the members themselves! Negotiation needs to involve elements of persuasion as well and every manager has found (sometimes to his or her cost) that it is as important to negotiate a deal *inside the organization* as it is *outside*!

Some participants on seminars recount horror stories of how much more difficult the internal negotiations actually are than the external ones. Negotiation, unfortunately, often gets mixed up with issues of authority and accountability.

Similarly, we can all recount tales of powerful organizations who have (mis)used their power to obtain an unusually advantageous deal from an opponent – only to discover later that it was unenforceable because the other party had gone into liquidation! What price enforceability now?

CASE HISTORY: PENALTY CLAUSES

A contractor was keen to gain one of three pilot contracts for a public authority for a major works project – divided into three geographical areas. In a highly competitive market the tenderer priced the proposal as keenly as possible – and was awarded part of the work. However, when all the costs were assembled, the contract ran at a loss and even threatened the financial stability of the contractor. The contract contained various clauses enabling retrospective claims to be made and, *as a matter of negotiated agreement*, the contractor was enabled to recover some of its unexpected costs overrun. **Collaborative relationships extend beyond the tendering and contract drafting process; sometimes negotiators need to help a supplier or client out of real difficulties!**

GREED

Many people can be readily tempted with thoughts of how a large lottery win could change their lives. The odds against winning do not seem to stop people playing and so it can be that negotiators fall for this – one of the most dangerous of commercial sins! Greed causes people who think they have spotted the 'main chance' to get rich, to buy/sell all the product in the hope of cornering the market. Sudden market changes may lead to desires to cancel/sell to another party (who is now prepared to buy at an even higher premium) and everything may seem fine until the bubble bursts.

Distortions in markets do happen from time to time in all walks of life, but periods of heavy demand usually precede periods of famine and it can take a long period before steady growth will rise again. (A good illustration of this lies with UK residential property values which rose at a phenomenal rate before a substantial crash – resulting in many householders holding negative equity. This situation was unheard of in peace-time and brought a sharp decline in economic activity in all the professions and trades related to house purchase.) Skilled negotiators have a watchful eye and concern for the future, whilst making the most of immediate opportunities.

MURPHY'S LAW – IMPLEMENTATION FAILURE!

So, if it can go wrong . . . it will! Greedy negotiators sometimes fail to have their agreements implemented – but never find out why! Only rarely do situations occur when a 'good faith' deal goes seriously wrong and attempts are made to hide the truth. Mostly, excuses are made for non-implementation which are plausible and unlikely to lead to the other party checking up. For example, it may be said that:

- *'A fire at the factory destroyed all the stock.'*
  Which factory? Where? Whose stock? What alternatives exist? What compensation will be available?
- *'The business has been taken over.'*
  The new management wants to make a profit from continuing in this market? If so, how will the take-over affect its policies? When/how will we find out?

- ■ '*Recent re-organization has changed all our levels of authority.*'
  You'll need to see my new boss to renegotiate this deal; alternatively, you could write direct to Japan/America/Korea!
- ■ '*Since we have committed ourselves to a quality system, all our contracts are being delayed by four weeks for checking and evaluation.*'
  Ultimately, this will be in everyone's interest but time is of the essence in our market – who shall we speak to to speed things up?

ACHIEVING THE BETTER DEAL FOR THE FUTURE

When all else fails, discreet enquiries around the market may reveal the extent of disruption. If it looks as if you are the only individual/organization to suffer these 'problems', perhaps you should ask yourself who you have managed to upset – and how? (The chart which follows illustrates the important relationship between implementation failure and credibility!)

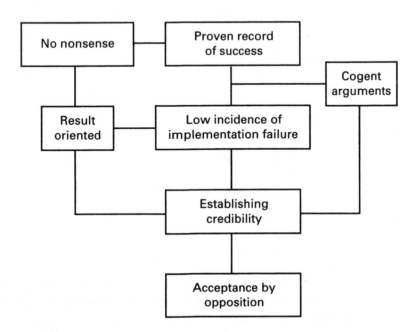

Most importantly, you may need to enter into a new round of negotiations to restore the status quo and rebuild a reputation of trust and integrity. Alternatively, it might be time to find another role! Either way, revising the whole process from the beginning of this book will not come amiss! Our final chapter also gives some advice on how to use the concepts of 'lifelong learning' to achieve even better deals in the future.

REVIEW ASSIGNMENT: ROGUES' GALLERY

The following case histories are offered for discussion and the reader should be able to propose a way out of the dilemmas.

CASE A: THE RENOVATION DEAL

At the time when new televisions were both expensive and scarce, a government surplus retailing business negotiated a deal with an owner/driver contractor to supply a large, defined quantity of renovated televisions with deliveries spread over a 12-month period. The deal was freely negotiated on both sides – the retailer eager to have a supply of televisions which it could easily sell at a substantial profit, the owner glad to have a large contract which guaranteed 12 months' work. Within a fortnight of the running of the contract, the contractor realized that it would be quite impossible for the renovation rate for the sets to be met. He contacted his customer to request a rescheduling of the deal.

How would you advise the parties involved?

CASE B: FLEXIBLE ROSTERING

A major trade union was approaching the annual negotiation round with a predictable list of objectives. The management team had been seeking productivity improvements for several years and, once again, sought the introduction of flexible rosters (incorporating split shifts). The salary benefit offered was viewed as highly attractive by the union negotiators who readily accepted the offer and signed up to the deal. The members themselves were horrified, so the proposal was put to a ballot.

How would you advise the management team and the union negotiators if the ballot rejected the offer?

CASE C: THE LEARNING ORGANIZATION?

A major retailer invested substantial sums in revamping its central distribution depot as a contribution towards increasing throughput and productivity of the facility. Amongst other changes, new pallet racking was installed. One of the firm's buyers negotiated a highly attractive deal with a supplier – achieving a substantial cost-price reduction in return for bulk packaging (as opposed to unit packaging). A chance lunchtime conversation between the buyer and the manager of the distribution centre revealed that the new 'bulk packs' would not fit into the new bays.

How would you advise the three parties involved?

CASE D: INTERNATIONAL NON-VERBAL COMMUNICATION

The fact that 'foreign national negotiators' look identical to 'home nationals' (i.e. they have a head, two arms and legs etc.) may leave us all with the impression that their thinking processes are identical to ours. When opponents are negotiating in a foreign language *for them* (i.e. in English), what signals might indicate emotions other than those which can be identified from verbal interactions?

Two colleagues in an international PR organization had been negotiating together – in English – seemingly establishing a sound, collaborative relationship with a win/win deal achieved. As the 'players' relaxed afterwards over a coffee they were talking in their own language; Yolande reacted

sharply to something George said to her and, using exceptionally aggressive body language, stalked off.

How would you advise a negotiator seeking evidence of
integrity when negotiating with opponents in a foreign
country?

CASE E: THE 'THROW-IN' SERVICE

A major British exporter won a substantial order for the
supply of materials used in the electrical industry – with an
exceptionally satisfactory negotiation meeting all round. At
the end of the meeting the Buyer requested the inclusion of an
additional, exceptional service involving the supply of 'cut
lengths' from the British factory. The exporter was only too
pleased to help – as part of the overall deal – expecting the use
of the service to be infrequent. Unbeknown to the Sales
Director involved, the customer cut back on their own staff
and passed all requests for cut lengths direct to the UK,
creating unacceptable work demands (and labour/cost pressure) on the British factory.

What steps would you take if you were the Sales Director
who concluded the deal?

CASE F: SETTING THE PACE FOR MODERN STANDARDS

A British manufacturer decided to set new standards for the
packaging for their products which had previously been supplied on cardboard reels. The 'preferred' European standard
was for the product to be prepared in hanks and then loaded
into the delivery lorry. With much publicity the firm promoted
the new service but, when the orders were fulfilled, the hanks
fell apart on the lorry.

What steps would you advise the company to take?

A similar situation arose when a leading retailer revamped its
'new' distribution centre and, on advice, included many state-
of-the-art facilities. One of these was racking which was only

suitable for European-sized pallets which were hailed as the new standard at the time. Unfortunately they were one of the few organizations to adopt the new standard and nearly all deliveries had to be 'hand-balled' onto new pallets before being put into bulk storage.

How would you evaluate the original negotiation and what steps would you have taken?

12 Towards lifelong learning

KEEPING THE LEARNING PROCESS GOING

To repeat an earlier slogan, negotiating is, and should be, fun! The process of trying to achieve (even) better deals can be very challenging – and most of all through the application of subtlety.

A participant at the end of a seminar once asked the leader if he had ever trained salespeople. 'Of course', was the reply – no single group has a monopoly over knowledge or skill development. The delegate was incensed – 'No wonder I have been having so much trouble with them,' he said. 'Now I will display my attendance certificate on the wall so that they can see that *I have been trained too*!' Credibility in negotiation comes from what we do – as much as from what we know, and it is sometimes best *not* to communicate our precise capabilities or knowledge to our opponents!

This short chapter invites the reader to continue the development process through some simple action points. Together they will form a powerful set of **negotiator's lifestyle assignments** and should help keep the development process going.

Be yourself

Don't try to apply 'slick formulae' with which you are not comfortable! Performance improvement comes with practice and this is best achieved in no- or low-risk situations, initially.

Be discreet

Don't invite 'retaliation' by trying to achieve maximum change or dramatic results. Buttress small improvements by building them into your normal negotiating patterns – your existing 'partners' like you the way you are. Introduce change slowly and subtly.

Learn from your mistakes

We all make mistakes – skilful negotiators *avoid repeating the same mistakes* by learning from them and moving on.

LEARN FROM LIFE!

Life situations often have a moral for us in other situations – negotiating is essentially about how to handle people and we can practice the skills in many walks of life and everyday situations. Practise, evaluate, apply!

Negotiate with more experienced people

'Boxing above your weight category' is one way of improving your skills – we learn how to debate, argue and persuade by working with people who are better at it than ourselves.

Obtain objective feedback

If you find it difficult to obtain positive/objective feedback on your negotiating strengths and weaknesses, book yourself onto a negotiation skills workshop which provides video coaching – especially with practical exercises.

Look for feedback from your opponents

Don't expect miracles – or the complete truth, quite a few will try to flatter you. However, even that tells you something about how they might view you and your skills. Try to build up a full picture of how you are seen and compare this with other sectors of your life.

BECOME A SELF-DEVELOPER

Extend your reading and try to apply new ideas in everyday life. The following texts will help you.

FURTHER READING

General

Successful Negotiation in a Week by Peter Fleming (London: Hodder & Stoughton, 1992)
Managing Negotiations by Gavin Kennedy (London: John Benson and John MacMillan Business Books, 1980)

Thinking on your Feet in Negotiations by Jane Hodgson (London: Pitman, 1994)

Sales and Marketing

Negotiate to Close by Gary Karrass (Glasgow: Fontana, 1985)

Bargaining for Results by John Winkler (London: Heinemann, 1981)

Getting to Yes by Roger Ury (London: Hutchinson, 1982)

Getting Past No by Roger Ury (London: Business Books, 1991)

Personal impact and skills

Body Language by Allan Pease (London: Sheldon Press, 1981)

Assertiveness at Work by Ken and Kate Back (Maidenhead: McGraw-Hill, 1982)

How to Win Friends and Influence People by Dale Carnegie (London: Cedar, 1953)

Tough Talking by David Martin (London: Pitman, 1993)

Experiential Learning by D. Kolb (New York: Prentice-Hall, 1984)

Use Your Head by Tony Buzan (London: BBC Publications, 1974)

Industrial relations

The Effective Negotiator by Gerald Atkinson (Newbury: Quest Research Publications Ltd, 1975)

Effective Negotiation by Alan Fowler (Wimbledon: Institute of Personnel Development, 1986)

Conflicts – A Better Way to Resolve Them by Edward de Bono (London: Harrap, 1985)

Peacing Together by David Cormack (Eastbourne: Monarch Publications, 1989)

Leadership

Action Centred Leadership by John Adair (Aldershot: Gower, 1973)

Apollo 13 by Jim Lovell and Jeffrey Kluger (London: Coronet Books, 1995)

— *Appendix: review checklist*

This checklist is intended as an aid to the reader; it could be used as a final check to ensure that all areas of a forthcoming negotiation have been covered in the preparation and plan.

PLANNING

1. Have we identified our shopping list? And that of our opponents?
2. Have we planned the parameters for each objective (MFP/LFP)?
3. Have we projected our opponents' positions on these?
4. Have we prepared a strategy for obtaining movement?
5. Are we prepared to move from our opening position?
6. Can we link any issues?
7. Have we prepared a strategy for using recesses?
8. Do the parties have a need to be seen to be bargaining 'fairly'?
9. Could we use hypothetical argument? (For example, supposing . . .)
10. Could any sanctions or motivators be used as part of the bargaining process?

RESEARCH

11. Have we negotiated on this/these issues before? What was the outcome?
12. Are there any precedents? (Do we have to set one?)
13. Is the other party hoping to renegotiate an existing agreement? If so, why?

14. Is the purpose to tighten up an existing agreement?
15. Do we have sufficient time to reach an agreement and to implement it?
16. Is there commitment to this timescale – on both sides?

Trust and integrity are built up by

17. Not withdrawing unconditional offers once made.
18. Demonstrating willingness to bargain on any issue which has been accepted as negotiable.
19. Ensuring opponents do not lose credibility in the eyes of their own side.
20. Avoiding any trickery in the final agreement.
21. Ensuring the final bargain is implemented in that form.
22. Does our position have a central theme? For example:

Periodic increase/decrease?	Profitability?
Adjustment of distortions?	Exploitation of bargaining power?
Maintenance of status quo?	Effort/reward ratio?
Good employer/ee?	Good supplier/marketer?
Regional/national comparisons?	Parity and differentials?

OPENING AND DISCUSSION

Clarifying the other party's position

Do you make use of:
23. Researching atmosphere and information in contacts with the other party's staff?
24. Informal discussions in meetings unrelated with the current negotiation?
25. The 'grapevine'?
26. Putting yourself into the other party's position?
27. Asking them to clarify their position? Over and over!
28. Playing 'devil's advocate' in the meeting?

Modifying the other party's expectations

Do you ever:
29. Question: The other party's assumptions?
            Their 'basic facts'?
            Their conclusions?

> Any omissions in their arguments?
> Any major inconsistencies?

30. Amplify the weaknesses in the arguments?
31. Project the consequences of applying their ideas?
32. Put forward a broad picture of the results of applying their ideas? (Especially where these are negative.)

Undermining the credibility of the other party
Do you ever:
33. Undermine the confidence of the other party?
34. Persuade them to refer back their arguments to:
    > their management?
    > their team/side?
35. Set a fast pace of work which they find exhausting/ debilitating/sapping of confidence?
36. Refer back to the (better) skills/support gained from past opponents?
37. Relate results to the opponent's lack of skills/training?

Building up own position
Do you:
38. Deliberately try to minimize your own weaknesses?
39. Emphasize your own strengths in argument and position – especially:
    > benefits to them?
    > reputation and skills (endorsed by others)?
    > emotional appeal?

PROPOSALS

What tactics do you use to encourage movement from the other side?
40. Trial proposals?
41. Conditional proposals: 'If ... then ...'?
42. Linking issues?
43. Recesses and adjournments?
44. Progress summaries?
45. A 'sprat' to catch their 'mackerel'?
46. Pressurizing with deadlines, timescales, mealtimes etc.?

47. Diluting enthusiasm for their case by encouraging weak members to move their position?

How can you encourage a reduction in their commitment?

48. Changing negotiators to encourage movement/break deadlock?
49. Blaming unpopular scapegoats?
50. Softening the effect of the other party moving by sympathizing with them?
51. Emphasising the 'generous' concessions you have been prepared to make?
52. Covering possible loss of face with a smokescreen?

SUMMARIZE

Do you ever:
53. Use summaries to confirm the position?
54. Emphasize the attraction of settling now (avoid more argument/meetings/effort)?

CLOSING

Do you ever:
55. Use additional concession(s) to induce a close?
56. Close by 'splitting the difference'?
57. Confirm in writing – at the meeting?
58. Use the either/or close?
59. Make the final offer/position public?
60. Use the 'walk-out' to emphasise the last offer?

— *Index*